The First Use Of Enemy Armor in Vietnam

TANKS IN THE WIRE

The First Use Of Enemy Armor in Vietnam

TANKS IN THE WIRE

by
David B. Stockwell

Daring Books
Canton • Ohio

Published by Daring Books
P.O. Box 20050, Canton, Ohio 44701

Printed in the United States of America.

Library of Congress Cataloging-in-Publication Data

Stockwell, David B., 1954-
    Tanks in the wire! : the first use of enemy armor in Vietnam / by
David B. Stockwell.
    p.   cm.
  Bibliography: p.
  Includes index.
  ISBN 0-938936 70-0
  1. Lang Vei (Vietnam), Battle of, 1968.   2. Vietnamese Conflict,
1961-1975--Tank warfare.   I. Title.
DS557.8.L28S76 1988
959.704 '342--dc19   88-25735
                                                                      CIP

For A-101 and the MIKE Force.

Table of Contents

Foreword

Tanks in the Wire! is about a battle in Vietnam, which was in itself and in the overall scheme of things, probably relatively insignificant. However, what it tells us about success and failure in combat provides lessons which, as a nation, we should learn, and learn well. Army Chief of Staff General Douglas MacArthur, known for saying, "There is no substitute for victory," wrote in 1935:

> "...The military student does not seek to learn from history the minutia and technique. In every age these are decisively influenced by the characteristics of weapons currently available and by the means at hand for maneuvering, supplying and controlling combat forces. But research does bring to light those *fundamental principles*, and their *combinations* and *applications*, which, in the past, have been productive of success. These principles know no limitations of time. Consequently, the Army extends its analytical interest to the dust-buried accounts of wars long past as well as to those still reeking with the scent of battle.(1)

Many strategists of today have been critical of the U.S. military effort in Vietnam and have suggested that we in the military must again become masters of the profession of arms. They echo MacArthur while fearing we may learn the wrong lessons. Captain Stockwell's work is a significant contribution to the endeavor of becoming masters of the profession of arms. It also provides the casual reader a means of better understanding the war in Vietnam.

Tanks in the Wire! provides those lessons by looking at a small battle...the battle for Lang Vei...which was part of a bigger battle...the battle of Khe Sanh, which, in turn, occurred at the *psychological* turning point in the war...January—March 1968...immediately before and after the 1968 Tet Offensive.

Lang Vei and Khe Sanh were important elements in the ultimate North Vietnamese psychological victory. The North Vietnamese won the tactical battles around the Khe Sanh Combat Base—the battles for the District Headquarters and the Lang Vei Special Forces Camp.

And, even in losing the Battle of Khe Sanh itself, their ability to keep the "agony of Khe Sanh" on the front pages of the daily papers and on everyones' TV screens for two-plus months accomplished their psychological goal. As Clausewitz points out, tactical victories (and one could also say tactical defeats) are not ends, but means to ends. The North Vietnamese understood this, did we? The reader should ask, as he reads *Tanks in the Wire!*:

-Was there a reason for the tactical defeat at Lang Vei?

-Did we need to try and defend Lang Vei?

-What if we had declined to leave that group of brave men out there on the Lao border isolated?

-What might have been different?

If the answers are that the results could have been different, then the same questions, if asked of other similar engagements, might begin to unravel the strategic failures of Vietnam. Colonel Harry Summers and General William Depuy, among others, looked at the U.S. failure from the perspective of grand strategy and concluded that our national strategy was incorrect.(2) Edward Luttwak, however, makes the point that each of the strategic intangibles must be in balance:

An intellectual's prejudice would rank strategy in its various levels as *the most important* of the intangibles that go into the making of military power. But actually, strategic coherence is no more important than any other of the intangibles, for at least a modest adequacy in each of them is an absolute requirement of military success. Without *fighting morale*, there is no military power, but even high morale counts for little without at least a minimum of *trained skill*. Both are of little avail if *cohesion* is lacking, and all must be for nought if there is no *adequate leadership* to direct the fighting. And what high-morale, skilled, cohesive, and decently-led forces can actually achieve in combat will depend on the quality of their tactics.

If forces fight with the wrong tactics or simply defy tactics by attempting the unfeasible, all the other qualities will only multiply casualties...*Adequate tactics* in each facet of the fighting are therefore necessary, but they are not self-sufficient. If the *operational methods* of war that the tactics serve are fundamentally wrong in concept, there can be no success. Finally, even the best of operational methods combining valid tactics ably carried out by motivated, skilled, cohesive, and well-led forces will only make failure more agonizing when one or more of the levels of strategy prohibit success.(3)

The point of all this is: by looking at the why and the how of battles such as Lang Vei, it may help to analyze the links between tactics and the operational art which Luttwak talks about. *Tanks in the Wire!* makes these linkages come alive.

Finally, the reader should consider some very specific lessons from this battle. These are unity of command, security, and surprise. The Army's doctrinal manual of the time, FM 100-5 defined these terms:

Unity of Command

"The decisive application of full combat power requires unity of command. Unity of command obtains unity of effort by coordinated action of *all forces* toward unity of effort, by the coordinated action of all forces toward a common goal. While coordination may be attained by cooperation, it is best achieved by vesting a *single commander* with the requisite authority."

Security

"Security is essential to the preservation of combat power. Security is achieved by *measures taken to prevent surprise*, preserve freedom of action, and deny the enemy information of friendly forces. Since risk is inherent in war, application of the principle of security does not imply undue caution and the avoidance of calculated risk. Security frequently is enhanced by bold seizure and retention of the initiative, which denies the enemy the opportunity to interfere."

Surprise

"Surprise can decisively shift the balance of combat power. By surprise, success out of proportion to the effort expended may be obtained. Surprise results from striking an enemy at a time, place, and *in a manner for which he is not prepared*. It is not essential that the enemy be taken unaware, but only that he becomes *aware too late* to react effectively. Factors contributing to surprise include speed, deception, application of unexpected combat power, effective intelligence and counterintelligence, to include communication and electronic security, and variations in tactics and methods of operations."(4)

Examples of these principles of war being practiced correctly and incorrectly abound in *Tanks in the Wire!* The reader should look at these principles and if they were adhered to or violated, as that may tell him much about the battle itself.

A personal issue is the Marine refusal to execute their contingency plan for the relief of the beleaguered camp. This refusal followed their earlier refusal to relieve the District Headquarters when it was surrounded. I have always believed if unity of command had existed, those refusals would not have occurred. The reader should consider that question himself and reach his own conclusions. Frank Willoughby and I reached our own conclusions many years ago.

Finally, the reader should recognize and appreciate personal bravery by American fighting men. The soldiers at Lang Vei were just a microcosm of the American soldiers who fought in Vietnam. Much has been written and shown in the media about the "fraggings" and other unsoldierly behavior in Vietnam. The media would lead you to believe all Vietnam veterans are psychologically scarred and were against the war. *Tanks in the Wire!* shows the opposite. It shows brave American soldiers as doing what they were trained to do, unwilling to quit and willing to sacrifice everything for their comrades. We as a society need to learn these soldierly qualities from this book and any other sources available we can find.

As a participant in the Battle of Khe Sanh and a distant observer of the Battle of Lang Vei, I salute the brave soldiers depicted in this book who fought the first tanks in the wire in South Vietnam. Theirs was a lonely task.

> Bruce B.G. Clarke
> Colonel, Armor
> U.S. Army at Khe Sanh during the Siege

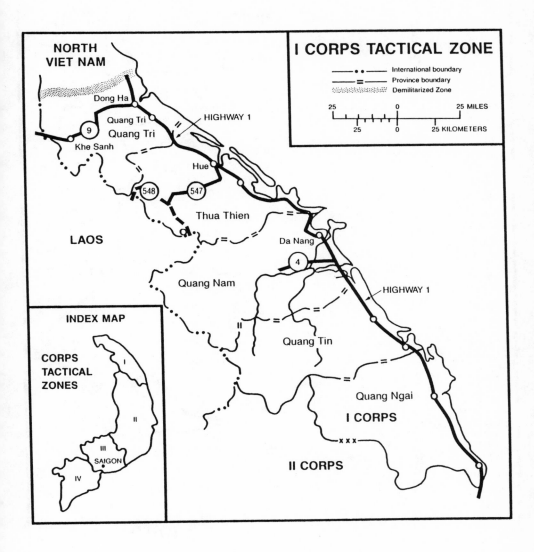

I CORPS TACTICAL ZONE

- •—•— International boundary
- —=— Province boundary
- Demilitarized Zone

25   0   25 MILES
25   0   25 KILOMETERS

NORTH VIET NAM

Dong Ha

Quang Tri

9

Khe Sanh

Quang Tri

HIGHWAY 1

Hue

548   547

Thua Thien

LAOS

Quang Nam

Da Nang

4

HIGHWAY 1

Quang Tin

Quang Ngai

I CORPS

x x x

II CORPS

INDEX MAP

CORPS TACTICAL ZONES

I

II

III

SAIGON

IV

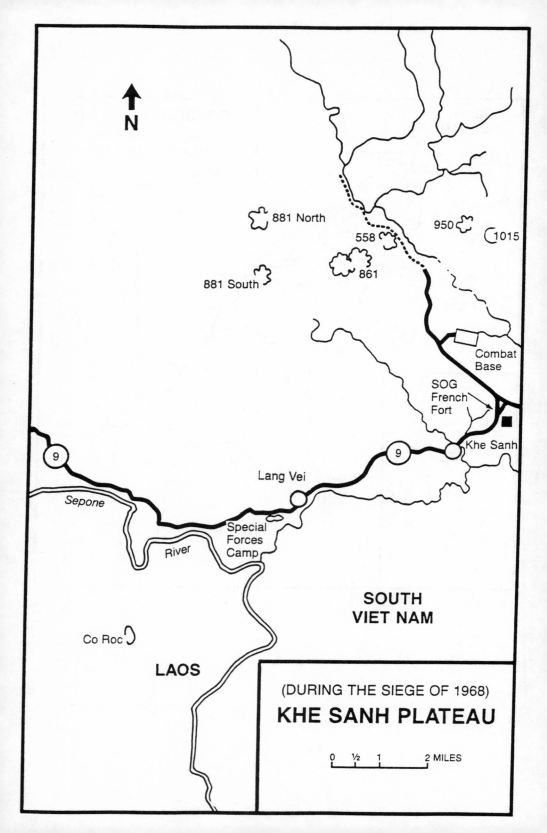

N

881 North

950   1015

558

861

881 South

Combat
Base

SOG
French
Fort

Khe Sanh

9

9

Lang Vei

Sepone

River

Special
Forces
Camp

SOUTH
VIET NAM

Co Roc

LAOS

(DURING THE SIEGE OF 1968)

KHE SANH PLATEAU

0   ½   1   2 MILES

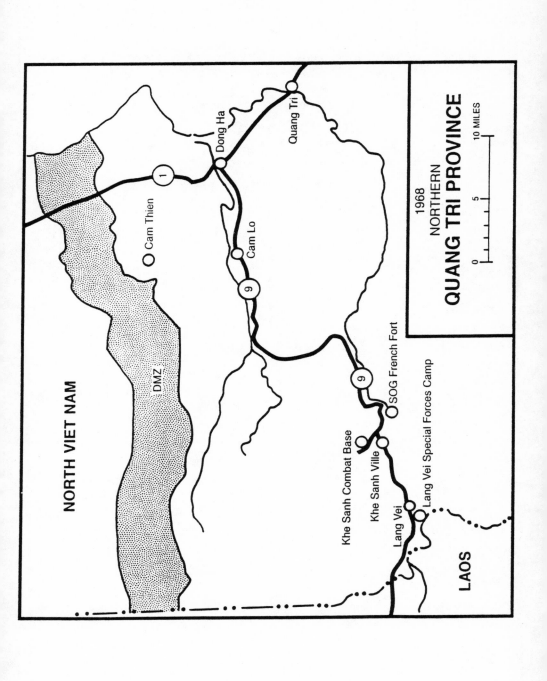

NORTH VIET NAM

DMZ

LAOS

1968
NORTHERN
QUANG TRI PROVINCE

10 MILES

0   5

Dong Ha

Quang Tri

Cam Thien

Cam Lo

1

9

9

SOG French Fort

Khe Sanh Combat Base

Khe Sanh Ville

Lang Vei

Lang Vei Special Forces Camp

Acknowledgments

Several people who helped me in the preparation of the manuscript require a salute.

Foremost are the soldiers who were involved in combat operations in and around Lang Vei from 1964 to 1968, and who talked to me. Many provided photographs, letters, maps, and editorial guidance: Colonel Bruce B.G. Clarke; Lieutenant Colonel Paul R. Longgrear; Lieutenant Colonel Jerry Crews; Lieutenant Colonel (Retired) Adam Husar; Lieutenant Colonel (Retired) Allan B. Imes; Major (Retired) James Whitenack; Major (Retired) Lee Dunlap; Captain (Retired) Paul Brubaker; Command Sergeant Major (Retired) William T. Craig; Command Sergeant Major (Retired) Mike Mielke; Gunnery Sergeant (Retired) Tom Gagnon; Staff Sergeant Tom Veneziani; Mike Perkins; and William Steptoe.

I also appreciate the help of my Vietnamese friends and interpreters, Duc and Van, and my Montagnard friend, Han.

My father, Lieutenant Colonel (Retired) Harvey L. Stockwell, who was an advisor in Hue from 1960 to 1961, provided a special insight to the early days of Vietnam that brought us closer. Thanks also to my brother, Lieutenant Colonel Robert L. Stockwell, who assisted with some of the research and provided encouragement.

The following individuals provided invaluable research and administrative help: Lovelea Usack; Captain Curtis Cheeseman; David Holt of the Patton Museum of Armor and Cavalry at Fort Knox, Kentucky; John Slonaker and Specialist Four Warsinske at the Institute of Military History, Carlisle Barracks, Pennsylvania; Danny Crawford at the USMC History and Museums Division, Washington, DC; and Ed Wolf, my "bus mate" in Sacramento, who read an early draft and provided editorial assistance.

I am especially indebted to Major James G. Johnson for his mapmaking skills, his probing questions, and his unyielding support.

Thanks to my wife, Sheryl, and my children, Corey and Amy, who encouraged me, and who inadvertently learned more about Lang Vei and Vietnam than they probably cared to.

Finally, thanks to an old Army buddy, Ron Hamme, who knows better than I do why I began the study of the battle of Lang Vei.

Introduction

The book you are holding in your hands is the result of idle curiosity and a labor of love. The author, an active duty Army armor officer, was perusing through his stack of books on Vietnam when he discovered a brief reference to a battle which, in itself, was small. The Battle of Lang Vei, as it became to be known, was obscured by the larger and more publicized Siege of Khe Sanh, to which it served as a prelude. It was generally overlooked by military and civilian historians as a significant event and relegated to the role as the scene of the opening shots for the Siege; the cursory mention it received would not have excited the interest of many casual readers.

What perked the interest of the author, though, was the mention that Lang Vei was the site of the first reported use of North Vietnamese armor against American forces. So, choosing this topic to be a subject of his continuing research, the author started collecting the exiguous material documenting this battle. His original idea was to publish an article for an Army trade publication. But, in the process of accumulating information, the scope of his work grew coterminously with the number of veterans of the battle who wished to contribute to it. In the end, the author had a corpus of material which would have required numerous magazine articles to deal with the subject matters fairly. He chose, instead, to write a book.

Tanks in the Wire! grew beyond the author's expectations. It grew because there is a story to be told and a lesson to be learned. The participants of the battle saw a chance to see themselves acting the part they played those years ago through different eyes and a different light. The battle didn't offer the participants much time for introspection. Now, when America seems to be going through the throes of its catharsis with the legacy of the Vietnam experience, individual veterans are trying to reassess their role in the drama and come to terms with their feelings and anger. Movies such as "Platoon" and the plethora of books that have pervaded the market help some and confuse others. This book means to do neither.

This book is a tale of U.S. Army Special Forces soldiers, Green Berets, fighting in a remote part of a country, in a remote part of the world. While America tuned in to their network television news broadcasts to see what was happening with the Siege of Khe Sanh and the status of the Tet Offensive, these and allied local militias had already fought their battle and many had died. It's a tale of heroism, valor, and courage. It's also one of terror and isolation. For one American participant, the battle became the catalyst for his spiritual conversion. More importantly, this book is a tale of American fighting men performing their duty regardless of the odds. While America agonized over the morality of her presence in Vietnam and the right to fight there, these men, secure in their own beliefs, fought the war and often died unknown. It is for them this book is written.

James G. Johnson
Major, U.S. Army
Federal Republic of Germany

Part I

1

"Tanks In The Wire!"

On the overcast morning of 24 January 1968, members of the 33rd Royal Laotian Elephant Battalion straggled east on Highway 9 for Laos toward the U.S. Army Special forces camp at Lang Vei.

The Green Beret camp, in the northwestern-most corner of South Vietnam, was eight kilometers west of the U.S. Marine Corps combat base at Khe Sanh and a scant one-and-a-half kilometers east of the border with Laos.

A huge American who looked like a fullback in season was blocking the highway as the Lao soldier who was leading the caravan approached him, took note of his rank, and greeted him.

"Hello, Lieutenant."

Paul Longgrear, the Special Forces lieutenant being addressed, gripped his rifle tighter and carefully surveyed the long gypsy band. *These people don't look very hostile, as a matter of fact, they look like they don't have much fight in them at all*, Longgrear thought. At least they're all walking. He nodded to the Lao soldier.

The Lao wore a patchwork combat uniform of tiger-striped trousers, a camouflaged shirt with American airborne wings and a ranger tab, and carried a Soviet-made AK-47 assault rifle.

"Who are you?" Longgrear demanded.

The Lao introduced himself as a lieutenant in the Royal Laotian Army who had trained in the United States and he identified his unit. Longgrear ordered his Mobile Strike (MIKE) Force soldiers to disarm the Laotians. The Lao pleaded with Longgrear not to take their weapons, especially the colonel's, his commander. "If he's Oriental," Longgrear said firmly, "and carrying a weapon, it goes on the ground."

The MIKE soldiers, Montagnard mercenaries from the tough Hre tribe, disarmed the Laotians as they approached, unsure of just who was friendly in that area. The MIKEs, who made their livings by collecting weapons from the victims of their attacks and receiving bounty payments from the Americans, sighed at the sight of the gleaming cherrywood stocks of the Soviet-made rifles the Laotians carried.

The women and children, some 2,200 civilians who followed their men in the tradition of poor field armies, pitched tents, drew water and prepared a midday meal while the Lao colonel went inside the Special Forces camp to confer with Captain Frank Willoughby, the camp commander of the 5th Special Forces Group (ABN).

The Lao colonel reported to the Americans that his unit had been hit two days before by North Vietnamese Army—NVA—soldiers less than ten miles west of Lang Vei near the village of Ban Houei San in Laos.

He said his position was overrun by two elements from the 304th and 325th NVA Divisions.

And he said tanks led the attack.

The information traded inside the Special Forces compound caused a sobering silence to descend on the command bunker and then quickly gave way to skepticism. "Where," the Americans wanted to know, "are your casualties? And why are your weapons in near-perfect condition?"

The Lao battalion soon left the camp and set up residence 800 meters east at a previous Special Forces camp, called Old Lang Vei, that had been overrun by Viet Cong troops eight months before. The Green Beret's questions to the Lao commander went unanswered, but his credibility "was about zero."

The Special Forces soldiers at Lang Vei had grown increasingly uncomfortable during the last few weeks. Dangling at the Vietnamese end of Highway 9, their mission of border surveillance had become cautious and then hazardous, as reported buildups of NVA troops just across the border in Laos erupted into frequent contacts with the enemy since Christmas. The Green Berets disbelieved the Lao claim of tanks, which had raised the ire of the battalion commander until, on 6 February, Lieutenant Colonel Daniel Schungel, commander of the Special Forces "C" team in Da Nang, flew out to meet with his Lao counterpart as a gesture of diplomacy.

Later on the 24th, news trickled down to the camp that earlier the same day, an Air Force Forward Air Controller (FAC) reported five enemy tanks in Laos as jets raced to support a special detachment operating outside of official boundaries. The airstrike resulted in one tank destroyed, and the others pulled off the road and managed to escape under the cover of the almost perpetual ground fog mists.

It was apparent something was going to happen—and soon. Was it possible the enemy had armored vehicles? The atmosphere in the Lang Vei camp had grown tense and the Americans had no patience for unsupported intelligence concerning the enemy, especially about tanks. They had to know what lurked in the fog-choked valleys to the west.

With nearly 8,000 noncombatants within a kilometer of his camp, including the Bru Montagnards of Lang Vei Village, all expecting some assistance, Willoughby radioed Da Nang for help. A six-man Special Forces team arrived the next day with ammunition, barrier materials, medicine and food. Willoughby had them refortify Old Lang Vei, inoculate the Bru and Lao children against cholera, and distribute powdered milk and other essential foods to the inhabitants of the crowded camp and village.

On 30 January, NVA Private Luong Dinh Du stumbled from the brush, strolled past the sleeping Bru soldiers guarding the gate of the camp, and emerged in the teamhouse doorway.

Tired Green Berets chatting at the teamhouse table glimpsed the enemy soldier clothed in his green uniform and pith helmet and carrying an AK-47—and clamored over one another to dive for cover behind the bar. The senior enlisted man of the Special Forces team, Sergeant First Class Bill Craig, cocked back a whiskey bottle to pitch at the soldier and then relented as Luong raised his hands; the NVA soldier simply wanted out of the war.

His unit, an infantry regiment in the 304th Division, suffered heavy casualties during a fight in Khe Sanh Village on 20 January. The North Vietnamese were forced back twice that day by a handful of U.S.

Marines and U.S. Army advisors. The friendly forces withdrew the next day. That battle, plus the terrifying B-52 strikes on his unit as it moved south along the Ho Chi Minh Trail in Laos, forced Luong to surrender. He "couldn't wait to trade sides."

Luong's unit was based from where the Lang Vei camp could be seen and during the night he slipped away and walked through the front gate, embarrassingly enough to the Americans, to give up.

The Special Forces soldiers wanted information on what he knew about tanks in the area. He said he didn't understand. They drew him a picture, literally.

He said he knew nothing of tanks, giving the Green Berets the impression that he was either "the world's best actor or he honestly did not know" about tanks just across the border.

Getting hard evidence of armored vehicles in the area was becoming a challenge, but Luong told his interrogators that an attack on the camp was imminent. Two days before, he said, his battalion executive officer and a squad of sappers—commandos—had reconnoitered the Lang Vei camp in preparation for an attack that was postponed for a second time for reasons unknown to him. The attack had not been canceled.

After a couple of hours of questioning, Luong was delivered to the Marines at Khe Sanh. In the hands of skilled Marine interrogators, he told of the unmistakable clanking of tracks accompanying his unit, although he had personally not seen the armored vehicles.

On the day Luong surrendered, a Green Beret patrol discovered a road built into the stream of the waist-deep Sepone River which marked the border with Laos. It was designed, they surmised, so the stream water could erase tire prints and preclude aerial observation. Still, they had no hard evidence that armored vehicles were poised to strike Lang Vei.

Willoughby felt if tanks were going to be used against his camp, they would most likely remain outside the defensive wire and provide fire support for infantry soldiers who would storm the perimeter.

Willoughby suspected if the enemy had tanks they would attack the 6,000-man U.S. Marine and South Vietnamese force at the Khe Sanh combat base.

Fearing the worst, they prepared for a possible armored vehicular assault. One hundred light anti-tank weapons—LAWs—were air-dropped into the camp. The one-shot, disposable, lightweight descendant of the famous Second World War bazooka was new to the MIKEs and the Bru, the local Montagnard tribesmen who comprised the Civilian Irregular Defense Group—CIDG (pronounced SIDGE), led by the Green Berets. The CIDG and MIKE soldiers were given classes and a few fired the weapons for familiarization.

Defenses at Lang Vei were hurriedly improved, although the 500-man camp was a veritable fortress. Having learned from their mistakes from the previous spring when the Old Lang Vei camp was overrun by Viet Cong, and with the help of U.S. Navy Seabees and their own fabled scrounging abilities, the Special Forces soldiers built a camp that only the strongest willed of the enemy would want to try to take.

Rows of heaped concertina and tanglefoot wire marked the perimeter and were interspersed with claymore mines, curved packages of death which propelled 750 pellets fired by a command detonated pound of C-4 plastic explosive.

Bunkers were reinforced with 8 x 8 timber that was almost impossible to get in Vietnam.

To raise the stakes, and because of the camp's precarious location at the end of the line of friendly outposts, Willoughby buttressed his force with support weapons and ammunition. The camp had two "four deuces" (4.2-inch mortars) with 800 high explosive and illumination rounds, two 81-millimeter and nineteen 60-millimeter mortars with 5,000 rounds of high explosive ammunition.

Willoughby also had two 106-millimeter anti-tank recoilless rifles with more than twenty high explosive rounds for each weapon. He placed one pointing down the southern road leading toward Lang Troai Village and the other on the western edge of the camp facing west on Highway 9. The camp sported four 57-millimeter recoilless rifles with almost 3,000 rounds of the flechette, or "beehives," anti-personnel variety.

Finally, the perimeter boasted two .50-caliber, two M-60 machineguns, and thirty-nine Browning Automatic Rifles (BAR).

Increased NVA mortar attacks on the Lang Vei camp ushered in the first week of February. Daily harassment of the camp centered

on the arrival of resupply helicopters, whose loads had to be hurriedly shed because of the threat of incoming mortar rounds. On the
afternoon of 6 February, some 30 or 40 rounds fell on the Green Berets
and their indigenous troops.

By this time, the Hre Montagnards on the observation point 800
meters west of the camp, who had disarmed the Laotian soldiers, were
incorporated into the camp defense, fitting in like puzzle pieces. Two
platoons of the MIKE company were on the perimeter and one platoon went out to the observation point at night.

There were difficulties getting the platoon members out on the night
of 6 February; they had apparently been spooked and shot at shadows
which they thought were NVA soldiers, and retreated back into camp.

Schungel saw the MIKEs scramble in through the gate as he returned
from a conference with the Lao colonel at Old Lang Vei. He wanted
to know what the hell was going on.

The two American Special Forces soldiers who accompanied them
claimed they saw nothing, but the Hre reaction was testimony to the
increased tension at Lang Vei. Longgrear, the MIKE company commander, eventually got them out to the observation point and then,
once the perimeter was checked, he turned in.

Forty-two minutes after midnight, eleven Soviet-made PT-76 amphibious tanks descended on the camp. The first five tanks drove up
a little used road from the south, which led from the village of Lang
Troai. Two of the tanks flashed their searchlights around at the
perimeter as two soldiers dismounted the vehicles and clipped the
chain link fence while the tank commanders observed almost casual-
ly in the cupolas. The tanks had tripped a stationary flare moments
before and while the vehicles were bathed in an eerie green light mixed
with swirling fog clouds, defenders from the CIDG Company 104
along that portion of the perimeter stared in disbelief—and then gunned
down the two enemy soldiers. The tanks buttoned up and bulled over
the fence toward the inner camp as Special Forces Sergeant Nick
Fragos hollered into the radio handset from atop the command bunker.

The radio in the room below him crackled to life with the startled
cry, "We have tanks in the wire!"

The battle for Lang Vei had begun.

2

"A Dirty, Disgusting War"— The Americans Take Charge

The Khe Sanh plateau had not always known war.

Long before the arrival of the American soldiers in the 1960s, even before their predecessors, the French soldiers, had carved their walled forts from the jungle in the 1950s, a French farmer named Eugene Poilane discovered this exceptionally rich land in the 1920s.

Poilane furrowed the soil and planted rich coffee groves ringed with clumps of avocado, jackfruit, and orange trees. Agriculturalists from around the world visited these rare gardens. Poilane described the plateau as a "place like Europe, with small valleys, plenty of water, and paths and flowers and hills, (with) land as good, as rich and red as in Tuscany."

The valleys throughout Khe Sanh were historically the hunting grounds of the Vietnamese emperors, where royalty stalked tiger, bear, deer, and panthers. Between the First and Second World Wars, wealthy hunters from America and France were lured there with the enticement of collecting for their trophy rooms.

Other French farmers took up residence at Khe Sanh and their lives, and their children's lives, flourished.

The indigenous people of Khe Sanh, the Bru, embraced the foreigners. The several hundred members of the Bru tribe belonged to a group of some 200 separate tribes who lived along the Annamite Mountain range that stretched 1200 miles through the spine of Vietnam. These tribes became known collectively as "the Montagnards,"

French for "mountaineer", whose separate unwritten languages, colorful tribal dress, and slash-and-burn agriculture earned them the label, "primitive."

The First Indochina War came to Vietnam in the early 1950s when French soldiers battled the communist Viet Minh forces. The Khe Sanh plateau remained untouched until a Viet Minh mortar attack killed a French woman and wounded Poilane in the leg in 1954.

Then the war went away.

In January 1962, two American Christian missionaries came to Khe Sanh. John and Carolyn Miller began to tackle the tasks of learning the Bru language, devising a written version, and then translating the Bible to convert these Montagnards to Christianity.

The Millers learned how vulnerable the Montagnards were when they bargained for their first home. One villager offered his home for sale for 8,000 piasters (about $130). The Millers, in the spirit of bartering at which Americans and the coastal dwelling Vietnamese were so adept, offered half that amount. The Bru villager became embarrassed and sold them the home at that reduced rate since that must have been all the Americans could afford.

The Millers met the French farmers at Khe Sanh whose knowledge of the area was so thorough, they charted the narrow foot paths in the mountains all the way to China. Soon they began to meet the ever-changing faces of the U.S. Army Special Forces.

On 8 July 1962, a U.S. Army Special Forces "A" detachment drove west on Highway 9 from the coast and established its military outpost at Khe Sanh. The team stopped at an old French fortification north of Khe Sanh Village and the highway, dusted out the old, cracking bunkers, leveled the small airfield, and recruited the Bru to lead them on long range patrols deep into the mountains of Laos.

The technique of training indigenous troops was called the "Civilian Irregular Defense Group." It was among the first in a series of Special Forces efforts to contain the remote border regions by providing reconnaissance and surveillance forces from those who lived there. These irregulars were thought to be more effective than the Army of the Republic of Vietnam—ARVN, or other Free World forces, because they lived in and knew the surrounding terrain.

The CIDG program became one of the answers to a new type of

warfare the U.S. forces faced in Vietnam. The Viet Cong—VC, had established its brand of terror tactics by slaying hamlet chieftains in remote areas for refusing to aid their guerrilla bands.

These unconventional fighters frustrated initial U.S. efforts to assist the ARVN. Lessons learned on the muddy European plains of the Second World War, where armies collided; or on the frozen Korean landscape during the conflict, where Asian adversaries attacked in human-wave, bugle-led throngs, did little to prepare U.S. advisors to counter the VC brand of terror.

"This," a U.S. Army Special Forces colonel said in 1961, "is a dirty, disgusting way to fight a war. If we could corner them in open terrain, we'd clobber all the Communists in 25 minutes. This way, it takes a week to find even 50."

The Khe Sanh plateau was beautiful. Nine shades of green were splashed on mountainous slopes criss-crossed with plunging crystalline waterfalls. But the plateau was also militarily important.

The French army recognized its importance in the 1950s and built forts along Highway 9 at Khe Sanh and even farther west to Lao Bao on the border with Laos.

The U.S. Army recognized that importance, too. Khe Sanh overlooked Highway 9, an east-west, all-weather road so far north and close to Laos, it could become a major enemy infiltration route if it was not checked. The Special Forces were tasked with surveillance of the border and Highway 9. Khe Sanh became the most endangered "A" camp in Vietnam.

So it was that the Khe Sanh plateau, rich in soil and richer still in military positioning, would become terrain later known for its combat "firsts." These "firsts" would lead up to one of the most controversial battles of the Second Indochina War, of which the tank attack on Lang Vei would become a pivotal part.

GREEN BERETS ARRIVE AT KHE SANH

U.S. Army Special Forces Captain Floyd Thompson arrived at Khe Sanh with his "A" team from Fort Bragg, North Carolina, in December, 1963. He and his team belonged to the 7th Special Forces

Group and began their six-month service in Vietnam.

Three months later, Thompson was a passenger in an L-19 reconnaissance fixed-wing aircraft observing the Demilitarized Zone, about 15 kilometers north of Khe Sanh and the Vietnamese border with Laos. The plane was shot down in Quang Tri Province, but the crash site was never found.

America had its first soldier missing in action.

Captain Allan Imes and his "A" team, A-728, replaced Thompson's team in May, 1964. One of Imes' missions was to determine Thompson's fate. After several months of questioning Montagnards throughout the area, many of whom claimed to remember the aircraft going down, Imes believed that although the crash site could not be found, Thompson could not have survived the impact.

Imes recommended in his tour after action report that Floyd Thompson should be declared killed in action.

Imes found the area around Khe Sanh to be relatively quiet, yet he knew the enemy was there. He met Poilane and the other French plantation owners and the Millers, who were nice enough, but he knew they were caught in the middle and must be paying the VC for the privilege of remaining there.

"One of the ironies of that war," Imes remembers. "They liked us, but paid them."

Imes' camp was built on what was left of an old French fort. Bamboo structures were erected around the camp for the CIDG to be housed. There were 500 soldiers in the forces, two-thirds of whom were Bru and the rest were Vietnamese recruited from Quang Tri and Da Nang.

Imes' "A" team was seasoned; several of the senior noncommissioned officers had combat experience from the Korean conflict. He also had three excellent Australians from the Special Air Service, "crackerjack" troops. Imes had the responsibility to patrol the border to detect/prevent infiltration by the enemy.

Contact with hostile soldiers during the early summer of 1964 was rare. The only casualties were mostly due to foot traps and boobytraps—and an occasional sniper. The patrols often had their worst fights with the terrain.

"It was rugged, rugged, tough terrain," Imes said. "The mountains were covered with very thick, heavy foliage. Sometimes we might go only 300-400 yards in one day due to the vegetation and steepness of the mountains."

When patrols were not out, Imes would drive his jeep over the rough road west and would sometimes visit the two American Special Forces advisors of an ARVN infantry battalion located at nearby Lang Vei. Highway 9 continued west from Lang Vei into Laos and was usable, but mined. None of the Americans ever hit a mine on the road and, except for that hazard, there was not much to fear.

A U.S. Marine reinforced platoon and Force Recon team moved into Imes' already cramped camp in the beginning of summer. The added firepower might have prevented an attack because nighttime listening posts reported occasional enemy probes, but the camp was never hit.

The Marines climbed the steep Tiger Mountain adjacent to the camp and emplaced a radio relay and a listening device which enabled them to electronically "look" into North Vietnam. Marines were not permitted to engage in combat patrols with the Green Berets.

"The Marines were not allowed to accompany us on operations," Imes said, "although we did manage to slip a few out with us. Had we all known what the future was to be, I don't think we would have worried about letting the Marines get a little combat experience."

Then, during the late spring when patrols were out, the VC destroyed eight of the nine bridges along Highway 9 east to the coast.

Aerial resupply became sporadic because of the low cloud ceiling, but when the aircraft did arrive, he made sure they contained the coffee beans of the French planters before they took off for the coast and a courtesy stop in Da Nang for the Frenchmen. With the highway out there was no way for them to get their coffee to market. Without that money, they might not be able to appease the VC for very long.

In August, Imes received word that two U.S. Navy destroyers had been fired on in the Gulf of Tonkin, the contiguous waters of North Vietnam. The U.S. Senate became outraged and extended war powers to President Lyndon Johnson with only two dissenting votes.

The picturesque plateau of Khe Sanh began to feel threatening to the Americans. They believed the bountiful area was a "good spot" for the enemy to stop over on its journey from North Vietnam.

Captain Allan B. Imes, driving, escorts US Army General Waters during an inspection of Imes' Special Forces camp at Khe Sanh shortly after the Tonkin Gulf incident in 1964. Waters told Imes that the North Vietnamese Army was massed beyond the hills in the background and would probably attack and overrun Imes' camp.

Photo courtesy of Allan B. Imes

General John K. Waters, commander of the US Army Pacific, consults with CPT Allan B. Imes and SFC Mike Mielke at the Khe Sanh Special Forces "A" camp shortly after the Tonkin Gulf crisis. His personal visit to consult with Imes, the "A" team leader, illustrates the strategic importance of the plateau. Waters gave the "A" team instructions to stay in the area and conduct guerrilla operations against the 20-30,000 NVA troops reportedly massed along the DMZ in preparation to overrun the camp in a push southward. Fortunately for the team, the attack did not occur.

Photo courtesy of Allan B. Imes

Patrols uncovered VC training facilities, bleachers, hospitals and barracks around Khe Sanh. They were crudely constructed, "but perfectly suitable for a temporary stay. We seldom found anyone home."

Vines with noise devices attached were discovered which, the Americans surmised, alerted the enemy to their presence, who would then empty the camps. The enemy didn't care if he was discovered, so long as he wasn't caught. They avoided big fights with the Americans so as not to spoil their good fortune.

But good fortune for the Americans had a way of turning sour—fast.

The lack of enemy engagements took a twist when Imes received a personal visit from General John K. Waters, commander of the U.S. Army Pacific. He brought along sobering news, but first wanted to see the situation at Khe Sanh for himself.

There were 20,000—30,000 NVA troops, Waters told Imes, massed north of the DMZ and ready to attack South Vietnam because of the Tonkin Crisis. If and when the attack occurred, Khe Sanh would be the first place overrun. Don't keep the indigenous troops together, Imes was told, but rather take command of the "A" team and recon team, and stay behind once the enemy passed. Stay and conduct guerrilla operations against the North Vietnamese Army.

Cautious patrols went out from the camp. In early November, just days before Imes and his team were to leave Vietnam, a patrol led by the Australians located a well-armed, well-equipped NVA company several miles to the northwest of the camp...in South Vietnam!

The patrol assaulted the North Vietnamese force and "shot them up pretty badly." They captured uniforms, German Mauser rifles and mortars, but there was no sign of the multidivision force poised to invade the south.

News of the engagement rocketed to Da Nang and higher Special Forces headquarters...the team was sure it was the first confirmed sighting of NVA troops in South Vietnam.

U.S. combat troops would not arrive in-country for several more months.

A Special Forces/CIDG patrol in 1964 near Khe Sanh found an NVA base camp where pungi sticks, razor-sharpened prongs of bamboo shown above, were made for later emplacement in booby traps. The enemy hastily abandoned their base camp moments before the patrol discovered it; empty cans dangling in the thick vines alerted them to the presence of the patrol.

Photo courtesy of Allan B. Imes

38

Two unidentified members of the Khe Sanh Special Forces "A" camp tag and display weapons and equipment seized after one of the camp's patrols ambushed a company of NVA soldiers in 1964 in South Vietnam, the first such contact by US forces.

Photo courtesy of Allan B. Imes

THE WAR HEATS UP

Anti-government protests rocked the northern part of South Vietnam early in 1966. U.S. combat troops had been battling the Viet Cong, but American military intelligence experts learned that General Vo Nguyen Giap, the North Vietnamese Army commander who handed the French a spectacular defeat in 1954 at Dien Bien Phu, planned to control the two northern provinces.

U.S. forces anticipated fighting the green-uniformed, pith-helmeted regulars in Thua Thien and Quang Tri Provinces.

General William C. Westmoreland, commander of U.S. troops in Vietnam, decided to strengthen Quang Tri Province just south of the DMZ, but he harbored no illusions that the enemy was not tough.

He found out just how formidable they could be in late 1965 when he sent the U.S. Army's 1st Cavalry Division into the gnarled canyons of the Ia Drang Valley after the Special Forces "A" camp there was overrun. The Cav was bloodied in that battle as it faced enemy regular troops, a foe who used "tactics and weapons which no one imagined they had."

NVA equipment hauls from that battle included the first AK-47 assault rifles and the first RPG-7 grenade launchers. The official number of U.S. soldiers killed in that autumn fight was 300, but most veterans who were there and were interviewed by correspondents wouldn't settle for less than three or even four times more than that figure.

Westmoreland decided to buttress the Special Forces effort at Khe Sanh. He had flown into the camp about twice a month in the fall of 1966 to receive briefings on the situation. Khe Sanh had become important to him from the first moment he saw it on an inspection tour shortly after taking command of U.S. Military Assistance Command, Vietnam—MACV.

He believed Khe Sanh "could serve as a patrol base for blocking enemy infiltration from Laos along (Highway) 9; a base for SOG (Studies and Observations Groups) operations to harass the enemy in Laos; an airstrip for reconnaissance planes surveying the Ho Chi Minh Trail; a western anchor for defenses south of the DMZ; and an eventual jump-off point for ground operations to cut the Ho Chi

Minh Trail." It was eventually used for each of these types of operations before the war was over.

The team of 11 Green Berets and their CIDG troops had found little evidence of the enemy near their camp. They had to go northwest and southwest as far as 15 kilometers to find the NVA, and even then they didn't find them in groups larger than squad-sized elements.

The camp had some South Vietnamese Special Forces, "but they were run-of-the-mill. They had one good NCO and the rest...avoided things." A definite plus for the camp was the three 105-millimeter howitzers from the 1st ARVN Infantry Division.

The only time the camp received fire was when one of the big 175-millimeter guns at Dong Ha supposedly fired a round into North Vietnam, but it impacted on the tip of the Khe Sanh runway.

Westmoreland anticipated that Khe Sanh would heat up. He told the Green Berets on one of his stops at Khe Sanh to expect some Marines to move in with them. The Marines arrived near the end of September 1966. The Special Forces and the Leathernecks got along well, initially.

One of the team's two executive officers, First Lieutenant Mike Perkins, was responsible for civic actions in the village. He was used to puttering around the village and French plantations in his jeep with his interpreter, and he took the Marine battalion commander to introduce him to the missionaries and the French.

The Leatherneck colonel immediately understood his role and helped soothe sore feelings between his unit and the inhabitants of the area by taking groceries to the civilians.

The poor relations occurred because the Marines had come to Khe Sanh from a "free-fire zone" elsewhere in Vietnam. In a "free-fire zone" everyone was a combatant. At Khe Sanh there were several hundred noncombatants, and the Marines suspected the peaceful villagers by day became snipers and ambushers against the Marines by night.

The Leathernecks' frustration at fighting an enemy they literally couldn't see, caused them to occasionally harass and threaten the Bru.

Perkins liked the Marine lieutenant colonel because he listened to the Green Berets; after all, they had been there a lot longer. The Special Forces had always maintained good relations with the local people.

A C-123 aircraft lands at the Khe Sanh Special Forces camp in August 1966. US Navy "Seabees" of the 33d Mobile Construction Battalion in the foreground arrived to begin replacing the runway's pierced steel planking with a new aluminum airstrip planking. The "Seabees" would later lengthen and reinforce the runway as the US Marine Corps 26th Regiment buttressed the camp into a combat base.

Photo courtesy of Mike Perkins

42

1LT Mike Perkins, the executive officer of A-101, prepares for a combat patrol in Vietnam. Perkin's team was displaced from Khe Sanh to Lang Vei in the fall of 1966 when the US Marines arrived on the Khe Sanh Plateau.

Photo courtesy of Mike Perkins

To the right front of the ¾-ton truck is the famous Khe Sanh "French Bunker." US Special Forces actually built the bunker in 1963.

Photo courtesy of Mike Perkins

The small Khe Sanh Special Forces camp begins to swell with the arrival of the 1st Battalion, 3rd Marines (US) in September 1966. The added fuel, vehicles, and living accommodations finally forced the Special Forces to relocate its camp in nearby Lang Vei three months later. The Marines would buttress Khe Sanh into a combat base that would house over **6,000** Leathernecks by the summer of **1967.**

Photo courtesy of Mike Perkins

US Marines post guard on a truck from the Khe Sanh Combat Base to the Lang Vei camp in December 1966. The road shown here went through the Poilane coffee plantation, and these Marines, from the 1st Battalion, 3rd Marines, helped the Special Forces soldiers relocate their camp shortly after the Marines arrived on the Khe Sanh Plateau.

Photo courtesy of Mike Perkins

"If there were any NVA in the area," Perkins said, "or if they were crossing the highway, the Bru would slow you down and talk to you. They'd tell you, 'don't go down this road.' If there was any NVA in the area the Bru would tell you."

Perkins was probably the best public relations man the Army had in the area. He was known as "bac si" (pronounced BOCK SHE), which means "doctor" in Vietnamese. He and his medic would drive down Highway 9 to the Laotian border and visit the small villas along the way—and take bandaids and antibiotics to the local people. He once took the Navy doctor assigned to the Marine battalion to the village of Lao Bao near the Laotian border without the colonel's permission.

They got stranded that night when a flash flood immobilized their jeep, and the Marine lieutenant colonel later reprimanded Perkins after the Marines sent trucks to recover the mired vehicle.

But the colonel knew that the public relations with the people couldn't hurt. He only wished he could convince some of his young Marine infantrymen of that. The villagers were tired of the Marines' continually sour attitudes toward them.

One day, Perkins passed a Marine patrol on the road as he was riding in his jeep to the village. He heard some shots about 300 meters past the patrol and went back. He found the Marines had been ambushed, but had only suffered minor leg wounds. He packed the wounded into his jeep and took them to the camp dispensary.

Later that day, he was in the village with his interpreter and met with the Bru chief Anha. The chief admitted his people had ambushed the Marines out of "grievance," not to kill, "but to mess them up a bit." Although Perkins could not agree with the chief's actions, he could certainly understand them. He realized the chief, who had served with the French and was imprisoned by the Viet Minh, "was on the short end of the stick" and would do what he had to do to keep his people safe.

The good relations between the Green Berets and the Leathernecks ended with the arrival of a larger Marine force at Khe Sanh in mid-December, 1966, which was commanded by a full colonel. The Special Forces were immediately moved out of their bunkers and into a tar paper shack erected overnight by visiting Navy Seabees. They went out on patrol shortly after that, and upon returning, found Marines living in their hooch. The "A" team and CIDG had been moved to nearby Lang Vei.

The new colonel, a "full bird" who outranked the battalion commander, did not acquire his subordinate's public relations expertise. "He strutted around the camp, a typical Marine colonel, and he made us wear our berets in the camp as though he just came from Parris Island," Perkins said. A misplaced sense of mission existed among the Leathernecks. A chaplain accompanying this larger force to Khe Sanh wrote, "This was a beautiful, if primitive, spot inhabited mostly by Montagnard tribesmen, their elephants, and assorted snakes and scorpions. It is difficult to say who looked more dejected, the Marines or the poor Special Forces we came to protect."

The new Marine commander had the Navy Mobile Construction Battalion (Seabee) lengthen the runway to Khe Sanh from 1500 to 3900 feet and cover it with lightweight, durable planking that was superior to the pierced steel type.

The new activity at Khe Sanh also attracted more Army attention. A Special Operations Group (SOG) unit arrived and settled into its own compound just south of Highway 9. The SOG unit established its compound around an old French fort which they dubbed, "Fort Dix," after the stateside post in New Jersey. They launched their "higher than secret clearance" missions into Laos from "Fort Dix" in a joint effort with the Central Intelligence Agency.

A visitor to the base surveyed the hum of activity and remarked, "It's like setting out honey to attract flies." "Flies" wearing NVA uniforms.

PREMONITION OF DISASTER—1967

The beginning of 1967 turned into a bad omen for the Green Berets at Lang Vei. U.S. F-4 Phantom fighters made a mistaken bombing run on the nearby Bru village on 7 March, cascading high explosive rounds and cluster bomb units on the families of the Bru soldiers. The troops on the ground fired starclusters—pyrotechnic signaling devices—and even machineguns at the jets as Special Forces soldiers

Typical Bru Montagnards at the Lang Vei Village in October 1966 peer curiously at an American photographer as he snaps their picture. The men from the village fought in the Civilian Irregular Defense Group (CIDG) that the Special Forces formed in 1962 until NVA tanks overran the Lang Vei camp in 1968.

Photo courtesy of Mike Perkins

Shards of freshly-bombed earth along Highway 9 mark the remains of Lang Vei Village. US Air Force fighter-bombers killed 125 Bru Montagnards in the village during a mistaken bombing run on March 7, 1967.

Photo courtesy of Mike Perkins

tried to reach the planes by radio—but could not find the proper frequency. Nearly 125 Bru civilians were killed in that attack and more than 400 were wounded.

Months of building up the trust of the local people was destroyed in less than 60 seconds.

A U.S. Army advisory team consisting of a field grade officer, an operations sergeant and a Vietnamese Regional Force company commanded by an ARVN lieutenant moved into the district compound in Khe Sanh Village to normalize relations with the civilians and advise the district chief.

The advisory team chief, Major James Whitenack, received a Marine infantry platoon to assist him and began piecing together the shattered relationship with the Bru.

Marine patrols north of the combat base began getting ambushed by NVA regulars in April. One patrol stumbled onto an enemy battalion digging into a hillside and the Leathernecks prematurely tripped an assault planned for the combat base. The Marines were reinforced with two infantry battalions and one artillery battalion of Leathernecks; they fought back.

Dubbed the "Hill Fights," the ensuing series of engagements took place on key terrain features north of the base. The hilltops became known by their elevation and relative position to one another, hills such as 881 North, 881 South and 861. Marine infantry units would soon "own" these hilltops to the north of the base in order to provide security for the bulk of the eventual 6,000 man force at Khe Sanh: the reinforced 26th Marine Regiment.

The Marines emerged victorious from these vicious, head-to-head confrontations with the NVA regulars during the "Hill Fights," but not before weaknesses were exposed in American tactics and weapons.

As the Marines took on the enemy, their new M-16 rifles began to break down. Congressmen began receiving letters from veterans of these fights, who claimed too many of their fellow Marines died with their weapons disassembled next to them as they desperately tried to dislodge a round stuck in the chamber.

The new $121-per-unit weapons were recalled and refitted with chrome chambers and a new buffer system to reduce the rate of fire. A laboratory analysis revealed that the gunpowder in the M-16 bullets,

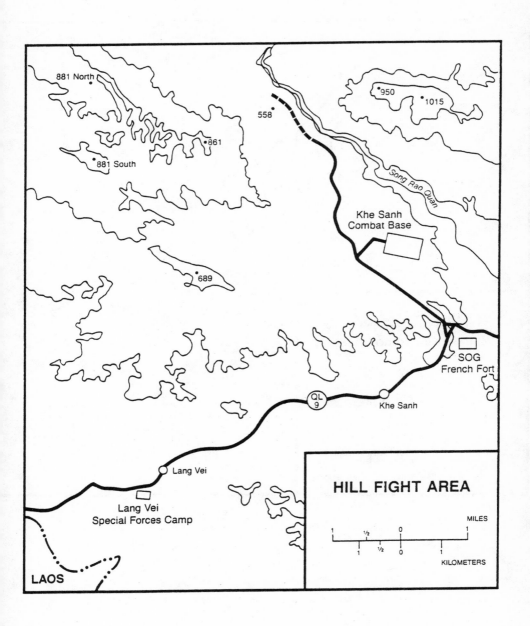

881 North

950
1015

558

861

881 South

Song Rao Quan

Khe Sanh
Combat Base

689

SOG
French Fort

QL
9

Khe Sanh

Lang Vei

Lang Vei
Special Forces Camp

HILL FIGHT AREA

MILES
1   ½   0   1

1   ½   0   1
KILOMETERS

LAOS

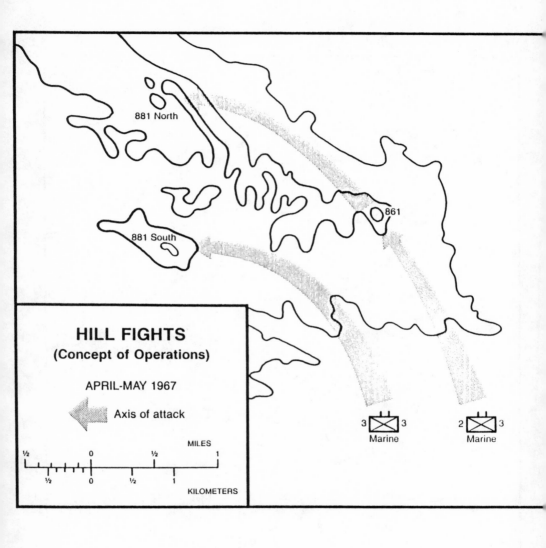

881 North

861

881 South

HILL FIGHTS
(Concept of Operations)

APRIL-MAY 1967

Axis of attack

MILES

½   0   ½   1

½   0   ½   1

KILOMETERS

3 ⊠ 3
Marine

2 ⊠ 3
Marine

a 5.56-millimeter projectile, caused excessive carbon buildup in the chambers of the rifles and jammed them. The replacement rounds shipped to Vietnam contained a different gunpowder to alleviate that problem.

Marine intelligence officers began tagging the enemy with unit IDs: they knew they opposed the 18th and 95th NVA Regiments, units already becoming known for their "outstanding camouflage, fire discipline, and aggressiveness."

THE "OLD" CAMP FALLS

Meanwhile, Green Berets patrols proceeded cautiously from Lang Vei. The team sergeant decided to keep his executive officer, First Lieutenant Stallings, in the compound, since he was days away from rotating back to the States. The brand new commander, Captain Crenshaw, was also advised to stay behind to learn the ropes from the command bunker. The team sergeant, Sergeant First Class Bill Steptoe, had his hands full with the constantly changing personnel inside the camp.

The "Hill Fights" were still under way on 4 May, when the 18th NVA regiment withdrew from Hill 861, while the 95th covered their withdrawal. While attention was diverted to the north, North Vietnamese soldiers cut the defensive wire on the south side of the Lang Vei camp and, aided by infiltrators in the CIDG, penetrated all the way to the command bunker at 0330 hours.

Major Whitenack and his troops were on alert that night in the village because of the heavy fighting to the north. He received a radio transmission from Sergeant Steptoe in the camp that he was the last American alive. Whitenack told his Vietnamese lieutenant to mobilize his force while he and his operations sergeant, medic, and radio operator sped off in his jeep for the camp.

They arrived just before first light—the NVA had already fled the camp.

Whitenack found Steptoe barely alive. He also found two other Americans alive in a communications trench. Steptoe thought they died when the roof of the communications bunker caved in, but they had escaped moments before. They were the only Americans to survive the attack.

Stallings had been hit with the opening shots of the fight as he exited the mess hall. A B-40 rocket exploded inside the command bunker wounding Crenshaw. An infiltrator ran up to the door of the bunker and finished him off with a burst of AK-47 fire. Once the wire was breached, the NVA swarmed over the camp, destroying as much as they could before leaving through a hole in the wire on the western edge of the compound.

In a classic adaptation of infiltration, Viet Cong soldiers assisted NVA units at Lang Vei by posing as CIDG recruits. One infiltrator taken prisoner after the battle confessed he had been directed to recruit other sympathizers among the CIDG once he had been accepted into the camp. He found four others to help him.

One man determined the locations of all bunkers in the camp; the second reported on all guard positions and how well they were manned; the third sketched the camp; and the fourth reported on all supplies brought in from Khe Sanh.

On the night of the attack, the original infiltrator and one of his recruits killed two of the camp guards and led the NVA through the wire into the camp's inner perimeter. During the 90-minute battle, 3 Green Berets survived; 17 CIDG were killed, 35 were wounded and 38 were reported missing. Enemy losses were 7 killed and 5 wounded.

This technique of prior infiltration was common to almost every attack on a CIDG camp and was almost impossible to stop.

The Green Berets hastened to escape the ghosts of their decimated camp and chose a hilltop 800 meters to the west. They left behind the striking image of gleaming white toilet bowls standing in the midst of blackened timbers, now called Old Lang Vei. The dogbone shaped plateau of their new home overlooked the border with Laos and Highway 9, and had better fields of fire.

Old Lang Vei as it appeared before the attack.
Photo courtesy of Shelby L. Stanton

54

Two views from the first Lang Vei camp looking northwest show Lang Vei Village in January 1967. Note the bunker and communications trench in the photo on the right.

Photos courtesy of Mike Perkins

The first Lang Vei camp looking north shows Hill 881S (the highest peak at the right center) which US Marines manned to protect the Khe Sanh Combat Base in January 1967. Marines at Khe Sanh occasionally helped the Special Forces soldiers at Lang Vei by providing some 105-mm artillery rounds (at the bottom of the photo) for the camp's one artillery gun owned by an ARVN unit. The ARVN gun and unit later left Lang Vei prior to the 1968 tank attack. *Photo courtesy of Mike Perkins*

Looking north from the center of the first Lang Vei camp is the USMC Khe Sanh Combat Base centered at the top right. An NVA force infiltrated the camp in May 1967 from the left portion of the photo and came up the trail through the wire that 1LT Perkins and SSG Osborne had cleared through a minefield in December 1966. *Photo courtesy of Mike Perkins*

Beneath the cloud cover at the top of the photo is the towering Co Roc Mountain in Laos as seen from the first Lang Vei camp. Co Roc housed NVA artillery that pounded Lang Vei and the USMC Khe Sanh Combat Base later in the war. The immediate hill in the background became the new Lang Vei camp after the first camp was overrun by NVA in May 1967.

Photo courtesy of Mike Perkins

Another view of the path that NVA infiltrators used in May 1967 to overrun the first Lang Vei camp. In December 1966, an airdrop of ammo and food landed in the camp's north wire (note the parachute in the background). 1LT Perkins and SSG Osborne cleared a path to the parachute bundle through an old ARVN minefield. That path was later used for watering parties from inside the camp, and also for the NVA infiltrators.

Photo courtesy of Mike Perkins

NVA forces overran the first Lang Vei camp in May 1967, partially shown here in January 1967. The hill in the background became the site of the new camp and the original camp was dubbed "Old Lang Vei." SFC Gene Ashley rallied a small group of Laotian soldiers at "Old Lang Vei" in five unsuccessful attempts to throw the tanks from the new camp in the 1968 battle. Ashley was posthumously awarded the Medal of Honor for his efforts.

Photo courtesy of Mike Perkins

Author Robin Moore took this photo of US Army Sergeant First Class William T. Craig as he takes a "breather" during a Special Forces patrol in Vietnam. Craig was the team sergeant at the Lang Vei camp during the tank battle in 1968.

Photo courtesy of Bill Craig

THE NEW LANG VEI—
"THE MOST MAGNIFICENT BUNKER"

This time, the Special Forces soldiers built a fortress.

A unit of Navy Seabees took up temporary residence at the new camp and, coupled with the fabled scrounging abilities of the Green Berets, "built the most magnificent bunker you ever laid eyes on."

The 8 x 8 beams of lumber which swung beneath the large helicopters in cargo nets was impossible to get in Vietnam...it must have all come from out of country.

The Green Berets built reinforced concrete bunkers and ringed their new camp with cyclone fencing, while the Marine combat base bunkers sagged from rotted timber supports. Dislikes between the two groups grew worse in the summer and fall of 1967.

In the fall of 1967, the SOG unit moved its headquarters from "Fort Dix" to a separate compound on the southwest corner of the combat base, and now called it Forward Operating Base (FOB) -3. The Marines distrusted the SOG, the CIA and the advisors in the Khe Sanh village and monitored their radio frequencies. The soldiers developed codewords to change radio frequencies so they could talk to one another in relative security.

It was becoming apparent that with the different units operating different missions so close to one another, and with each of them answering to separate higher headquarters, no single military commander on the Khe Sanh plateau had complete authority over all of the units.

One of the American principles of war is unity of command. Each of the higher headquarters which had units operating on the Khe Sanh plateau answered to a single commander, U.S. Army General William C. Westmoreland, several hundred miles south in the South Vietnamese capital of Saigon. On the Khe Sanh plateau, however, no single authority existed.

Marine commanders at Khe Sanh especially disliked the Green Berets, whom they called, "wretches," and felt they were a "law unto themselves."

Special Forces soldiers felt the Marines stumbled through the area in too large units with too little understanding of just how tough things

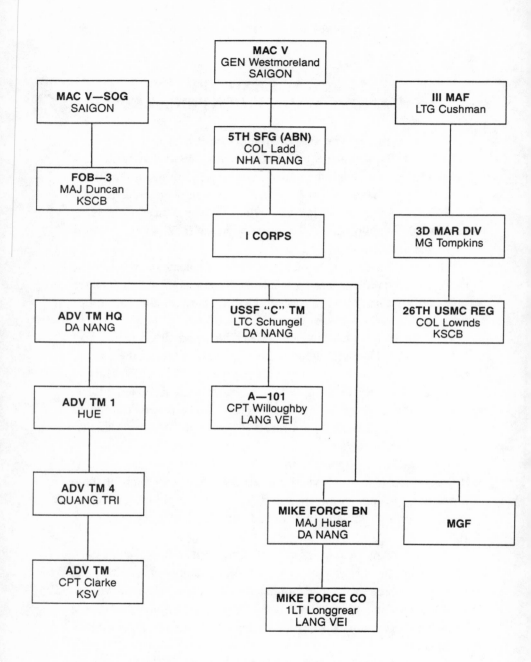

could get in the mountains near Laos.

Visiting Marine commanders were also upset because they knew the 26th Marines would be required to help bail out the Special Forces if they got into trouble with the enemy. One Leatherneck company rehearsed a dismounted, overland relief effort to the camp from the combat base which took them just over nineteen hours. Some Marine commanders did not believe the Green Berets were worth the effort.

The Green Berets were upset as well. Their operations in that area required them to rely on stealth. They discovered that not only did they operate outside of the protective artillery umbrella of the U.S. Army firebase at Camp J.J. Carroll to the east, they sometimes feared the Marines might mistake them for the enemy and call in airstrikes.

And they also believed the Marines reported areas cleared of enemy activity when, in fact, they had not patrolled in those areas.

In August 1967, a convoy of big 175-millimeter artillery guns was sent down Highway 9 to reinforce the Khe Sanh combat base's 105-and 155-millimeter pieces of the attached 1st Battalion, 13th Field Artillery Regiment. The convoy never joined the members of the 1/13 at Khe Sanh. An ambush sent them reeling back to the east to avoid a slaughter. The base would have to rely on its own guns for direct support, but could count on general support from the 175s at Camp Carroll.

FIRST TANK SIGHTING

Later that fall, intelligence experts glimpsed the first sign that infiltration was growing. A Huey helicopter (UH-1B) gunship from the 161st Aviation Company, attached to a unit of the 5th Special Forces Group (ABN) near Hue, was on a special operation along the Ho Chi Minh Trail in Laos adjacent to the southern end of North Vietnam. The pilot spotted an enemy tank, probably a thin-skinned Soviet-made PT-76, and fired his rockets at it. The door gunner, Sergeant Thomas Veneziani, spotted the rounds for the pilot and reported a hit. The helicopter dove and fired again, but the impacting rounds did not stop the tank. The helicopter had been in the air too long on its previously assigned mission and was, unfortunately, almost out of ammunition. The pilot radioed the report back to his headquarters and steered the helicopter back home.

In December 1967, a 196-man Mobile Strike Force company composed of Hre Montagnards, with an additional five Green Berets in command, was sent to strengthen the Lang Vei camp. Captain Frank Willoughby, the new camp commander, placed them on an "Observation Post," actually a mini camp, a half mile to the west on Highway 9.

The Special Forces kept a MIKE force unit poised in Da Nang to assist the camp in the event of an overwhelming enemy assault. The Marines were ordered to have two rifle companies ready to move by foot or helicopter to Lang Vei. Marine Colonel David Lownds, Commander at Khe Sanh, sent a forward observer to the camp to preplan artillery fires and kept two rifle companies on alert.

But Lang Vei was not high on Lownds' priority list.

3

The "Yards"—
Mountain Fighters

The mountain people of Vietnam are called Montagnards (pronounced MOHN-TAHN-YAR), French for, "mountaineer," who live in quiet villages in the highlands and practice slash-and-burn agriculture.

Montagnard is a generic term to describe the bewildering mixture of racial and linguistic groups and subgroups. Their number was estimated at 800,000 to one million.

The Montagnard no-nonsense, nonabstract view of life and the critical terrain they occupied made them ripe for exploitation. The urbanite Vietnamese could not thrive in the primitive setting of the highlands, yet the strategic spine of Annamite Mountains arching 1,200 miles through Vietnam proved critical for militarists. The Montagnards had recurring visitors.

A U.S. Army captain parachuted into the highlands in 1945 with a butterfly collection. He was welcomed by a hobbyist, guerrilla leader who was living among the Montagnards, molding them into guerrilla units to fight the Japanese who occupied Vietnam. The little known, middle-aged politician was Ho Chi Minh.

During the Second World War, Ho received American aid, mostly weapons and ammunition, from the Office of Strategic Services— OSS. He reciprocated by supplying the Americans with information about the Japanese and it was clear he was trying to woo the United States. Ho supplied the Americans in Vietnam with aides, many of whom, if not all, were Vietnamese communists.

When the Japanese were ousted from Vietnam in the fall of 1945, Ho's troops took Hanoi and Ho became the president of North Vietnam. "The presence of the American senior officers at Viet Minh functions and the flying of the American flag over their residence made it easy to convince the unsophisticated population that the United States had established official relations with the Viet Minh regime and was giving the revolutionaries its fullest backing."

An alliance, a true alliance, between the United States and the pronationalist (and pro-communist) Ho Chi Minh was not established. It is too simplistic to think that, perhaps if the United States had established a solid relationship with Ho Chi Minh, its combat involvement in Vietnam two decades later may not have occurred.

When the American captain parachuted into the highlands to meet with Ho, it was to fight a common enemy, the Japanese, with the use of a common ally, the Montagnards.

Ho was not the first to use the Montagnard villages for sanctuaries, nor the last to recruit the Hill People for revolution and rebellion. The Americans, who sought to align themselves with Ho against the Japanese, would use the Montagnards as well, only the next time, Ho's troops and American Special Forces would vie for their loyalty.

When the Japanese were ousted and Ho returned to North Vietnam as president, the French reimposed their domain in Vietnam, Cambodia, and Laos, and termed the area "French Indochina." Their relationship with the Montagnards was more regulatory than diplomatic. The French controlled the Montagnard land and issued ownership certificates only if the Montagnards applied for them. To the Montagnard way of life, a piece of paper legislating ownership of land was as useful to life as an unstrung bow was for hunting.

"Basically, the Montagnards are free people," a Montagnard official in the 1960s South Vietnamese government (GVN) explained. "They don't want people to control them, to ask them to do what they don't want to do...they are very free.

"They can cross the border into Laos, they can cross the border into South Vietnam, they can even cross the border into North Vietnam. They don't care about boundaries."

The French-imposed rule irritated the Montagnards. Some fell under the spell of the Viet Minh and joined the communists, and families were divided. The regime of South Vietnamese Premier Ngo Dinh Diem reinforced this control, but many Montagnards stayed in their villages because they believed the presence of the Americans would protect them against the brutalities of the communists. "We thought the outsiders would protect us."

The 1960s and American technology brought on a clash between the timeless hamlet philosophy of the elders and the technological lure of the future for the youngsters.

"The Montagnards?" an American foreign service officer in Saigon repeated to his interviewer. "They are caught in the middle, between the Vietnamese and (the Americans), between the Vietnamese and the Viet Cong, between animism and Christianity, between illiteracy and education...in one generation between a father who hammers iron to make a knife and a son who wants to study science."

The U.S. Army Special Forces soldiers understood the strategic importance of the sparsely populated highlands and worked hard to overcome cultural and linguistic differences with the Montagnards. The Americans started a military training school in Soa Cam, near Hue, to form the nucleus of the Montagnard cadre. They paid the Montagnards and introduced them to Pepsi-Cola and Salem cigarettes. But their indoctrination included more than commodities.

The Special Forces donned the Montagnard tribal dress, struggled to learn the village customs and separate, unwritten dialects, and earned metal bracelets of friendship that adorned their wrists. These outreaches became more than just gestures of manipulation, they produced a genuine affection that threatened the Americans with an affliction known as, "going native." One Special Forces sergeant with the Montagnards was captured by the Viet Cong in 1962, but was released a short time later as a gesture of diplomacy. He returned to the Montagnards and his forearm boasted many more bracelets than did the wrists of his peers.

These outreaches on the part of the Americans meant something special to the Montagnards. "The Vietnamese never did that. The Montagnards (thought of the Special Forces), 'Oh, they want to know us, to like us.'"

The Viet Cong never did that either. The VC terrorism in the

Montagnard hamlets included the public executions of the chieftains if they did not agree to VC demands. Their brutal recruitment of the Montagnards did yield some conscripts, but the relationship between the two groups was tempestuous and never as positive as between the Montagnards and the Americans.

The Office of Montagnard Affairs began in the early 1960s as an affirmative action organization in Hue. Its political orientation made it responsive to the office of the prime minister, despite the military training of Montagnard cadre nearby. Cadre leaders learned reconnaissance techniques that would enable them to lead Special Forces on long range "look-see" patrols through the highlands into the jungled mountains of Laos.

The Special Forces established its northwestern most outpost in Khe Sanh in August 1962 and recruited their Montagnard force from among the members of the Bru tribe. The Viet Cong assassinated the chieftain of Khe Sanh Village and the 4th Battalion, 1st ARVN Infantry Regiment was sent to Khe Sanh to provide security for the Special Forces in this most distant corner of South Vietnam near Laos.

After the assassination of Diem in November 1963 and the overthrow of the South Vietnamese government; the Office of Montagnard Affairs, now composed mostly of military leaders, moved to Saigon and shifted from control of the prime minister to the Minister of Defense. Montagnard moderates felt the office should be separate from any other, with its own structure, military forces and flag. The camp at Soa Cam shifted its training of Montagnards to ARVN troops, who longed to become South Vietnamese Special Forces (VNSF), or LLDB for the Vietnamese title "Luc Luong Dac Biet."

The Montagnards felt the GVN who replaced Diem would improve relations between the Hill People and the South Vietnamese. Shortly after being moved to Saigon, the Montagnard organization became FULRO...Front Unifie de Liberacion de la Race Oprime; the United Front for the Liberation of Oppressed Races. FULRO lobbied for its own schools, university scholarships for Montagnards and quotas to support those scholarships. These demands cluttered the in-boxes on the desks of GVN officials and rumors of a Montagnard revolt against the GVN surfaced in September 1964, barely a month after the Tonkin Crisis launched the United States into a combat role in Vietnam.

The Montagnards were not the only political group in South Vietnam that was dissatisfied with the government. Buddhists, whose immolations on street corners had immense emotional impact on the rest of the world and who once wanted "Diem's head...and not on a silver platter, but enveloped in the American flag," did not cease their public suicides with Diem's assassination. The post-Diem, self-inflicted deaths by fire did not receive the publicity they had previously, and led the public to form the belief that the conflict between the Buddhists and the Catholic Diem were not religious after all, but politically motivated protests.

Diem had made a catastrophic mistake. He ended the 500-year tradition of village chief elections and instead, made appointments to those posts. Many of these appointees were outsiders to the villages and the Viet Cong used this situation to full advantage.

Between January and October 1964, 500 government officials were kidnapped from villages and hamlets by Viet Cong terrorists. These kidnappings were presumably for "re-education" and the individuals were probably sent back to the villages to administer for the VC. A similar number were not so fortunate...they were taken out and executed.

The villagers gave the Viet Cong a "Robin Hood halo" for these assasinations.

*   *   *

The American advisory role in Vietnam expanded to include training for their counterparts in the ARVN. For example, when the American Special Forces started its Vietnamese Special Forces training camp at Soa Cam, the intent was that the VNSF would train the indigenous Montagnards how to fight the communists and the U.S. Green Berets would advise the VNSF. It was training of the "learn one, do one, teach one" variety and worked well in theory. Differences, however, between the Vietnamese and Montagnards often meant that the Americans had to step in and take charge of the indigenous troops.

News surfaced in the summer of 1964 that a Montagnard revolt was brewing and American Special Forces officers took it to heart. On 19 September 1964, three flares were shot into the night air, exploded into burning light and drifted to earth on their tiny parachutes, signaling the start of the Montagnard revolt near Ban Me Thuot. Montagnard antagonists in 5 Special Forces camps near Ban Me Thuot (Ban Don, Buon Brieng, Buon Mi Ga, Bon Sar Pa and Bu Prang) killed 29 VNSF, captured a hundred more and seized 20 Americans as hostages.

The Montagnards in revolt were from the Rhade tribe, and the American Green Berets in charge of them quelled the rebellion by sheer will, through the rapport they had established.

A council of Rhade leaders at the "A" camp at Buon Brieng held a religious ceremony to determine the gods' guidance for them, and the "A" team leader, Captain Vernon Gillespie, donned the tribal dress along with the Rhade leaders; he became part of their ceremony. The gods "told" the leaders they must not rebel, and the notion of armed conflict against the Americans and the South Vietnamese Special Forces quickly subsided.

Gillespie's brave actions helped soothe exposed nerve endings, but not before throats went dry in Saigon.

The rebellion was finally vanquished when the commander of the Special Forces in that area, the III Corps region, Colonel John Freund, who spoke fluent French, ended the fight with words and not bullets by taking a firm stand against the rebellious Rhade...a stand backed by fighter planes circling overhead that persuaded the Montagnards to desist. It worked.

The Special Forces' difficult mission to recruit and train indigenous troops was forever tempered. The Montagnards' survival meant the possibility of shifting loyalties to whomever held the high card of military strength, or in some cases, money, in that area.

Besides, some Montagnards in key political positions felt that the Americans presence was temporary, that the American actions spoke louder than their words.

"Look at their tin huts and sandbags," they said. "The Americans will not stay in Vietnam."

4

"Volcano Under the Snow"— The Enemy

Vo Nguyen Giap was born in 1912 in a small village just north of the 17th Parallel. The son of a precolonial scholar who opposed French rule, Giap was born to a nation locked in a centuries-old struggle with outside forces.

Chinese invaders from the north had entered in force and departed intermittently for more than a thousand years. War had become congenital to the Vietnamese, and so had the human virtue of patience and the tactical virtue of surprise.

One of the leaders who came in the 13th century was Kublai Khan, grandson of Ghengis, who stormed southward and set up residence in Hanoi. The Vietnamese waited for the tropical diseases to brew among their invaders—which sent the Chinese staggering back home.

When the Chinese returned in 1787, Vietnamese soldiers hid in caves for more than a year and then infiltrated into Hanoi on the eve of Tet, the Lunar New Year celebration. Nguyen Hue, the Vietnamese army leader, had caught the Chinese intoxicated during the holidays and sent the superior force reeling north across the border.

Giap had become an ardent student of war and of politics. But before tactical sense, he would first develop a political subconscious by flexing his dissention biceps against the French. He joined the underground as a student at the Lycee National Academy in Hue where he led demonstrations. Giap was arrested and sentenced to three years imprisonment, but was released after a few months for good behavior.

Giap met Ho Chi Minh while planning these protests and formed an alliance with this straw-thin man with the wispy beard, who had changed his name several times before settling on one he hoped would achieve worldwide notoriety. American intelligence officers described Ho as a "half-starved Santa Claus" and cried, "It's damned difficult to go out and tell people to hate a guy who looks like that."

Most Vietnamese believe Ho's original name was Nguyen Tat Thanh, with Nguyen being the family name. Although he had perhaps a dozen aliases, his two most common were Nguyen Ai Quoc and Ho Chi Minh. They were chosen for their significance in Chinese ideographs, the former meaning Nguyen, the Patriot, and the latter, Ho, the Enlightened One.

When he was in Canton in the 1920s, Ho's names were less profound; Ly Thuy, Lee Suei and Vuong Son Nhi were all ideographic wordplays on one another. His whereabouts in the 1930s are unaccounted for, which lead to speculation that there was more than one Ho Chi Minh. The London Daily Worker, dated 11 August 1932, carried an account of his death in a Hong Kong prison under the name of Nguyen Ai Quoc. It was also rumored he died in a Soviet prison. In either case, myths arose that he was replaced by an unknown who went on to rule North Vietnam.

No other leader in the world has been as enigmatic as Ho Chi Minh, who refused to clarify his past in order to capitalize on the mystery. Over the years, he gave the world contradictory explanations, which his followers believed was behavior befitting a good leader.

Ho disguised his Marxist leanings beneath a cloak of nationalism, convincing the world he sought to unify an independent Vietnam. Giap developed the same burning fanaticism for Marxism and for revolt against the French who occupied his country, and was nicknamed, "Volcano Under the Snow" by Ho for his calm exterior that concealed his seething emotions.

Giap received his law degree from French Indochina's single university in Hanoi in 1937, with high marks in political economics. He married Ming Thai, the daughter of a former professor and, turning away from his journalism skills; as a young man he published anti-French newspapers; Giap found a position as a secondary school teacher. His colleagues chuckled as he outlined Napoleon's campaigns for his students on schoolroom blackboards. "Do you want to become a general?" they teased.

His wife publicly echoed his anti-French sentiments, and she and her sister were arrested. Giap's sister-in-law was guillotined by the French and his wife died of disease while imprisoned.

Giap continued his allegiance with Ho and in October 1944, formed the country's first national army unit under Ho's guidance. His "Armed Propaganda Brigade" was actually little more than an understrength platoon consisting of 34 men of the first Viet Minh force and armed with 2 muskets, 17 rifles, 14 flintlocks and a Chinese pistol.

Two months later, on 22 December, they attacked two isolated French outposts near the northern border with China and massacred the garrisons.

Ho Chi Minh became president of North Vietnam in September, 1945, and began to deal with the French to undermine the political opposition of his own countrymen, few of whom suspected his alliance with Moscow.

As Giap, now General Giap, took his military strategy from the table to the battlefield, Ho worked his diplomacy beneath the table, handing the French the names of prominent individuals whom, he said, had opposed their rule. They had, in fact, opposed Ho Chi Minh.

Once the French neutralized Ho's opponents for him, he would point the finger at the Europeans and claim they were undermining the nation.

Giap learned his military strategy at the expense of his men. His army, the Viet Minh, had swelled into the tens of thousands who rallied to the cause of ousting the imperialists. He lost 6,000 men in one day in "human-wave" attacks against the French. He lost 9,000 men another time in North Vietnam's fertile Red River Delta.

Giap mentioned such losses with indifference. "Every 2 minutes 300,000 people die on this planet. What are thousands for a battle? In war, death doesn't count."

The French became victims of their own confidence as they parachuted into the Vietnamese valley of Dien Bien Phu in 1954, which was near the border with Laos. Paratroopers, Foreign Legionnaires, Morrocans, Algerians—15,000 total—fortified the French garrison on the valley floor, which was ringed by high ground.

A French artillery column was crushed by the Viet Minh as it moved north to support the defenders. Giap's laborers pushed his patchwork hundred-piece artillery: American, Soviet and captured French guns, by hand up the mud-slick slopes of the high ground surrounding Dien Bien Phu. Coolies strained behind the 440 pounds of rice and munitions straddling each bicycle in their convoys and grunted up the hills.

After 100 days of preparation and reconnaissance, and of an artillery overmatch guaranteed by the ambush of the French column, Giap began pounding the garrison which lay below him.

For 56 days the French forces were bombarded by weapons they had not imagined the Viet Minh to have. Previous victories taught them they could win face-to-face encounters with their Asian adversaries. Giap learned that, too. Five thousand soldiers of the French force perished in the battle of Dien Bien Phu.

The cocksureness of the French paratroopers at Dien Bien Phu began to evaporate with the loss of supplies. Giap relied on the strong backs of his coolies to supply his troops in combat. The French dug heavily fortified positions, but in the thick of the fighting looked skyward to receive airdropped supplies. They watched in dismay as bundles of repair parts, medical equipment and wine attached to parachutes drifted over their heads toward the delighted shouts of the enemy.

Near the end of the siege the Frenchmen lost their resolve. The artillery commander for the garrison committed suicide. On 7 May, 10,000 soldiers of the French forces surrendered. Giap was hailed as a military genius, as the Asian Napoleon, for his use of pure, orthodox 18th century siege technique.

Giap's writings on warfare were studied in military colleges throughout the world. They echoed the strategy of his predecessors, men such as Marshal Tran Hung Dao, who patiently waited for bacteria and viruses to claim the legions of Kublai Khan. Dao believed any invader could be defeated by lengthening a war from months to years, from years to decades.

"Time is always in our favor," Dao had written in military journals studied in later centuries by his countrymen, who regarded him as the Clausewitz of the Far East and of equal military importance as China's Sun Tzu.

Surprise was also in their favor.

"Surprise," Giap said, "is a very important factor in war. To use surprise to defeat the enemy is a major problem in military art. It is the art of catching the enemy by surprise as to the direction, targets and time of our attack, the forces fielded and the forms of combat used by our side.

"We must use surprise in the most varied ways."

The Viet Minh dashed the last resolve of the French forces in Vietnam with the ambush of a highly mobile, regimental task force: Groupement Mobile 100.

GM 100 was one of the best light infantry units of its type in the First Indochinese War. The unit was based at An Khe in South Vietnam's Central Highlands along Highway 19 and was ordered to keep the highway open. This major road runs east to Qui Nhon and the South China Sea and was considered to be a vital link between the coast and the highlands.

The Viet Minh, having mopped up Dien Bien Phu, looked southward to the highlands and GM 100, the elite group of battle-hardened veterans; many of whom were attached to the U.S. Army's 2nd Infantry Division during the Korean Conflict and wore the American white star and Indianhead patch on their right sleeves to indicate combat service.

On 24 June, the column left An Khe to move to Pleiku on orders from the French High Command, acknowledging that the Viet Minh now owned most of Highway 19.

As the column passed the Mang Yang Pass, situated about halfway between the two cities, a Viet Minh ambush erupted and swarms of enemy soldiers stormed the column. The single day battle was a slaughter.

After the Geneva Accords between France and Vietnam the following month, French soldiers buried their compatriots from GM 100 atop the Mang Yang Pass in graves dug so the dead would forever stand and face toward France...2,000 graves filled with lime, over which the grass has never grown.

By the spring of 1967, Giap had fought the Americans for two full years. The ranks of the People's Army, successors to the Viet Minh and known to Free World forces as the North Vietnamese Army— NVA, had swelled from 250,000 active duty soldiers in 1965 to almost

400,000 in 1967.

The larger force was needed to answer the call to battle in South Vietnam, but the new soldiers did not fear death because of a lack of training. The Party had increased its control over the militia and reinforced its ideological guidelines by introducing political commissars into each military unit; tactical training expanded to include night fighting skills.

Political indoctrination became an essential ingredient in the Party's recipe for a People's Army soldier. Troops rallied beneath Ho Chi Minh's banner of national independence by chanting his three point battle cry: "Defend the North, Free the South, Unite the Country!" They etched, "For Nation—Forget Self" onto their hats. They listened to war stories about national heroes, told by the political cadre in training camp social gatherings, and which increased their enthusiasm.

Upon being sent south, a soldier's pay was given to his family for the first few months to reconcile his loved ones. If wounded, the soldier received free medical and rehabilitory care. If killed, the soldier's burial expenses are paid by the state and his children receive a small pension. Medals, honors and titles are bestowed upon the dead to console his family and reinforce patriotism in the community.

Soldiers were taught to be wary of spies among their own people in the south, that fighting spirits dissolve beneath the lure of money and pretty girls. Ho explained these premises, and the need to constantly reinforce them, to farm youths-turned-soldiers in poetic terms: "Revolutionary ethics do not come from the sky. They are consolidated through daily, persistent cultivation, like a pearl and like gold. The more a pearl is polished, the brighter it is, and the more gold is smelted the purer it becomes."

Soldiers were also taught to be wary of one another. They were formed into trios called Three-Man Cells. Each cell was composed of a buddy team plus one extra soldier. They were told to assist one another if sick or wounded and to participate in discussions, where the other two in the cell would analyze their mistakes and reinforce battlefield camaraderie.

The Three-Man Cell also protected the army against desertions. One man may run away, he may even talk his buddy into deserting.

But three men become a bit suspicious of one another and do not know when their sagging enthusiasm might be reported by their comrades to higher authorities.

Unit political commissars were more than cheerleaders. They supervised ideological training and outranked tactical field commanders. A North Vietnamese company commander who defected in 1966 explained the relationship: "The influence of the Party Chapter is of the utmost importance because the Party is the absolute commander. Every military plan or project has to be inspected by the Party Chapter.

"If the project was approved, the Party Chapter would make a resolution to give it back to the commanders, who will execute and realize the plan in the name of the government. On the other hand, if the Party Chapter wasn't pleased with the plan, the commanders had to change it."

Giap had monitored French morale at home during the First Indochinese War. He became fully aware of eroding French support and of American hesitation to commit U.S. troops in a "colonial" war. Giap's decision to liquidate the French before the arrival of American material aid was gauged by readings on this homefront political barometer.

Giap now monitored the political commitment in the United States and believed Americans did not support the war.

By 1967, he felt American military leaders, "overestimated their strong points." He estimated less than one tenth of the half-million American fighting force in Vietnam aggressively patrolled the countryside on any given day.

Giap believed his troops possessed, "an unshakable conviction that their cause was just." American troops rotated home after a year in Vietnam; North Vietnamese soldiers received no trips home until the war was over. Many American fighting men were draftees; the Party was "reluctant" to conscript men, realizing that revolutionary fervor was paramount to military success.

Instead, the Party persuaded mothers to encourage their sons to volunteer, publicly praised these women as heroes to "The Cause," and lauded these "voluntary" soldiers.

Sensitive that despair can fill the void of a son gone to war, the Party ordered family members at home to organize into Self-Defense

Forces. Under the slogan, "Every Citizen a Soldier," this militia was given the mission to "protect local areas" with a variety of support tasks designed to assist regular troops and to instill a feeling that the entire family was participating in the war effort.

In every manual and speech to his troops, Giap emphasized camouflage, deception, surprise and misdirection. The North Vietnamese soldiers were reared with the land and learned its many uses in combat.

Truck drivers, departing North Vietnam for the arduous trip south along the Ho Chi Minh Trail, first attached freshly cut foliage, palm fronds and banana leaves to their vehicles to avoid aerial detection. Jeep drivers wove leaves into fishnet webbing stretched over their carriages and transportation depots were constructed to resemble tree-laden parks.

As U.S. bombing efforts along The Trail increased in 1967, the drivers moved with greater dispersion so as not to attract the attention of aerial reconnaissance aircraft searching the jungle for convoys, and frequently drove in total blackout for several nights at a time.

The B-52 Stratofortress, the American super-bomber aircraft, hindered traffic moving south by the use of bombs called Destructors, which would not detonate until struck by a vehicle creeping along the road. But they could not stop the convoys.

By December 1967, enemy troop and supply carriers streamed into the area of Laos adjacent to northern South Vietnam in record numbers.

Always, Giap and Ho emphasized the need for high quality training for its soldiers. Elite troops received a year of intensive commando training to learn the many uses of explosives. They learned to pinpoint and vigorously lead ground attacks by breaching the outer layer of protective wire with demolitions.

On graduation day, they became "dac cong" and basked in the praise of commencement speeches delivered by Giap and Ho.

Giap unfolded his strategy for war in the northern provinces of South Vietnam in 1965. Regiments of green-clad NVA troops clashed with the U.S. Army's 1st Cavalry Division in the Ia Drang Valley, a North Vietnamese sanctuary. This was the second battle between U.S. and NVA soldiers, the first having occurred a year before near Khe Sanh

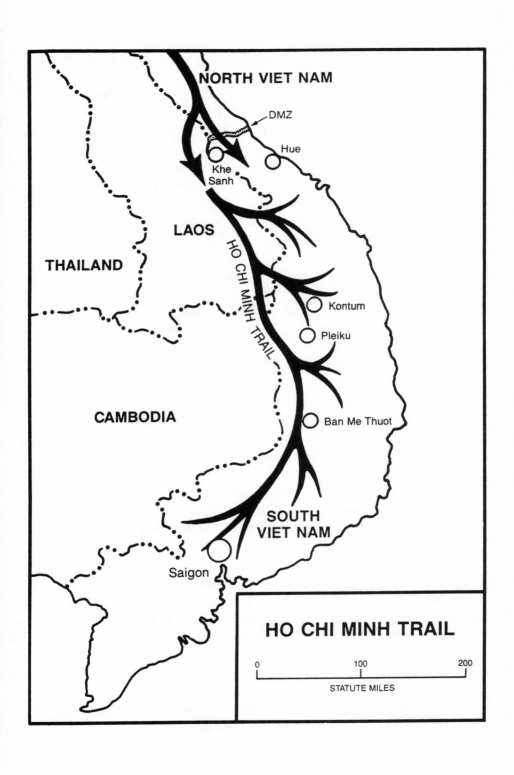

NORTH VIET NAM

DMZ

Hue

Khe
Sanh

LAOS

THAILAND

HO CHI MINH TRAIL

Kontum

Pleiku

CAMBODIA

Ban Me Thuot

SOUTH
VIET NAM

Saigon

HO CHI MINH TRAIL

0   100   200

STATUTE MILES

when a U.S. and Australian Special Forces patrol shot up a company of regular troops shortly after the Tonkin Crisis. The NVA lost in Ia Drang, but had shocked Americans by their appearance in force in the south.

Special Forces camps became a favorite target of the North Vietnamese Army. A U.S. Green Beret twelve-man "A" team was fortified with a similar South Vietnamese Special Forces team and several hundred indigenous troops in each camp, situated far from the secure base areas, but buttressed with weapons and bunkers into mini-fortresses.

The 95B and 101C NVA Regiments attacked the Special Forces camp in western Thua Thien Province's A Shau Valley in March 1966. The camp was overrun by North Vietnamese and abandoned by the Americans, which allowed the NVA to build sanctuaries and major logistical bases and to construct roads into Laos to intersect with The Trail. This handhold permitted the infiltration of five divisions by the end of 1966 into the heavily foliaged and gnarled ravines of the A Shau. It brought the total number of NVA in the south to more than 280,000 troops, augmented by an additional 80,000 political cadre.

Sophisticated equipment also surfaced. The Special Forces camp at Khe Sanh was attacked in January 1966 with 120-millimeter mortars which had almost twice the range of previous mortars.

Viet Cong and local guerrillas began ambushing U.S. forces with Chinese Communist copies of the Soviet AK-47 assault rifle. They used the lightweight RPG-2 rocket-propelled grenade launcher with more frequency than when first seen in 1964.

The northern provinces were rocked in mid-1966 by anti-government protests led by the Struggle Movement of militant Buddhists. Particularly hard hit was Hue, the traditional cultural center of South Vietnam.

U.S. analysts interpreted this as an attempt by Giap to sever Hue from the south, impose an occupational army demarcation through the Central Highlands from Laos to the coast, and use the northern provinces for future negotiations.

The shift to NVA regular troops in the south appeared to Free World forces as the third and final phase of North Vietnam's theory of revolution, as seen against the French a dozen years earlier.

"Our strategy," Giap said during the First Indochinese War, "early in the course of the third stage is that of a general counteroffensive. We shall attack without cease. During the first and second stages, we gnawed away at enemy forces. Now, mobile warfare will become the principal activity; positional and guerrilla warfare will become secondary."

Giap had not counted on U.S. ability to provide mass and maneuver through the birth of the helicopter as a warhorse and he lost his bid to slice off northern South Vietnam as a bargaining chip.

In the summer of 1967, Giap decided a significant battlefield victory would be a prerequisite for peace talks. For six months he toiled over his general offensive, supervised his staff and polished the details.

Giap concluded three things. The first phase of the offensive would send coordinated ground attacks against Free World forces and installations in remote areas to draw out U.S. and South Vietnamese troops from their defensive positions around the cities. The second phase would bolster his attack on major cities. The third phase included a major thrust east on Highway 9 from Laos to the coast to capture or destroy Free World forces in northern South Vietnam and enhance North Vietnam's position at the bargaining table.

Reaching into his country's rich military past, Giap decided that the attack should commence as Nguyen Hue's attack had against the Chinese almost 200 years before: on the eve of the celebration of Tet, the Chinese Lunar New Year.

5

The Tet Offensive

Several weeks before the People's Liberation Armed Forces and elements of the Vietnam People's Army began their synchronized assaults against virtually every city in South Vietnam, the order for battle was published.

The order, in the form of public announcements and newspaper articles in North Vietnam, spoke of "an historic campaign ahead." It urged "very strong military attacks in coordinations with the uprisings of the local population to take over towns and cities...(soldiers) should move toward liberating the capital city (Saigon), take power and try to rally enemy brigades and regiments to our side, one by one. Propaganda should be broadly disseminated among the population in general, and leaflets should be used to reach enemy officers and enlisted personnel...(but) do not specify times for implementation."

A press release published by the Joint United States Public Affairs Office—JUSPAO, credited an element from the 101st Airborne Division with discovering an enemy document boasting this bold plan. For the first time in history, an attack order for a major offensive was publicized in advance by the side to be attacked...25 days before it was to happen.

United States intelligence experts operating in Vietnam did not realize the specifics of the plan. They did not know the enemy, planning and moving in secret, was carrying supplies on bicycles and on the backs of its coolies to organize the fight. They didn't know the enemy was planning on striking more than 100 cities and towns to include Saigon, 39 of 44 provincial capitals and 71 district capitals. They didn't know Hanoi would pitch 67,000 of its soldiers...nearly one-fourth of its force in South Vietnam...at the 1.1 million Free World troops.

The enemy hoped their adversaries would be scattered too thinly in the face of sudden assaults on every front and could not mass and maneuver. They planned that the government of South Vietnam would be paralyzed and caught off guard. They planned the attack on the holiday of the Lunar New Year, Tet, when South Vietnam was at a cease fire.

American intelligence experts discounted the information they possessed. Few had heard of Nguyen Hue, the Vietnamese Army commander nearly 200 years before, who attacked the Chinese occupying Hanoi on the eve of Tet and sent the superior force reeling north across the border.

In lieu of specifics supplied by the captured document, an all-out offensive against South Vietnam seemed incredibly unlikely. There were other signs, such as the massive troop buildups across the border in Laos at the northwestern corner of South Vietnam, that would support the idea of some type of attack. These signs, which focused on the reinforced regiment of U.S. Marines at Khe Sanh and the Special Forces camp at Lang Vei, were believed. But the very boldness of an engulfing offensive seemed too fantastic to believe.

After all, the U.S. command was reducing its estimates of the enemy troop strengths in order to show we were winning. Outlandish claims of strength by the enemy had occurred before, but those were attempts to bolster sagging morale. Perhaps this talk of impending victory was a desperate maneuver by the communists in the face of almost certain defeat; "considering the high costs and risks involved, the idea of nationwide urban attacks for political and psychological gains seemed implausible."

General William C. Westmoreland and his assistant chief of intelligence differed on their predictions of when the enemy would strike. Westmoreland believed it would probably occur before Tet, his staff believed it might come after Tet. No one suspected it would come during the Lunar New Year holiday itself.

Intelligence officers believed the attack would occur at Khe Sanh. The buttressing of the Marine Corps regiment there was conducted to lure the enemy out of the mountainous crags surrounding the jungled plateau of Khe Sanh and to their certain deaths. Comparisons between Khe Sanh and the defeat of the French at Dien Bien Phu were first made in private, and then in staff meetings at the very highest levels. Preparations were made so that Khe Sanh would not become another Dien Bien Phu.

But the likelihood that the enemy would attack every city in South Vietnam was remote. "If we'd gotten the whole battle plan," a senior intelligence officer in South Vietnam said of the Tet offensive, "it wouldn't have been believed. It wouldn't have been credible to us."

* * *

Radio reports and secret teletype messages woke up Westmoreland on 23 January with urgent requests for bombers, cargo ships and soldiers. But the requests were not for combat in Vietnam.

The USS Pueblo, an intelligence-gathering seacraft, was seized during the night by North Korean troops in international waters off the coast of that country. The helpless crew of the ship was being paraded before television cameras, accused by the North Koreans as being spies.

Westmoreland's defenses in Saigon and the central Highlands were stretched thin so he could concentrate his forces in the northern two provinces. He couldn't afford to lose resources.

The case was worsened when the South Korean government asked the U.S. for the return of its crack "Blue Dragon" Brigade, on duty with American forces in Vietnam.

Westmoreland trusted the South Korean soldiers more than the ARVN, and he had them guard the sprawling airbase and support complex at Da Nang, the northern-most seaport in South Vietnam. He wanted the South Koreans to guard his rear areas while he battled at Khe Sanh, and now those plans were threatened.

The possibility surfaced days later that the start of Tet and the seizure of the Pueblo were coordinated attacks. A North Vietnamese military aid delegation visited North Korea in August 1967, after the plans for the general offensive had begun. It was not known if the Vietnamese told their plans to the Koreans and asked them for a diversionary attack, but the thought seemed plausible.

*   *   *

The reported buildups of enemy troops in Laos adjacent to Khe Sanh in December 1967, caused Westmoreland to order massive concentrations of intelligence gathering equipment to be strewn around the plateau. Seismic and acoustic sensors were kicked out of the open doors of flying aircraft and plummeted to the ground. These experimental sensors provided early warning of troop concentrations by electronically alerting airborne crews circling in the skies overhead.

Intelligence officers pinpointed an area inside Laos believed to be the site of the North Vietnamese Headquarters for the Khe Sanh assault. B-52s furrowed the ground in this area the weekend before the Tet offensive began with tons of high explosive bombs, and the North Vietnamese command radio net ceased to broadcast.

Those who believed in the similarities between Khe Sanh and Dien Bien Phu conjectured that the NVA commander, General Vo Nguyen Giap, was in Laotian headquarters to personally take charge of the Khe Sanh battle. Images of Giap standing in the mouth of a cave giving orders to his subordinate field commanders, as in the photograph taken of him in preparation for Dien Bien Phu, seemed possible. Giap had become legendary in the eyes of the Americans of whom one European journalist said, "...they inflated him themselves, with their mania for legends...You frighten children by whispering, 'I'll send for the boogeyman.' You frighten Americans by whispering, 'Giap is coming.'"

When the bombs rained on the Laotian headquarters, Giap was in Hanoi tending to the final details of the upcoming general offensive to commence on the eve of Tet.

*   *   *

"In preparation for the New Year, everyone should work to be lucky.

"To begin Tet, the New Year celebration, with good luck means to have good luck all year. One should start the new year by wearing only new clothes and all one's debts should be paid. Your first visitor should be someone lucky, with many sons, so that his luck will rub off on you.

"Cut a sprig from an apricot tree, and if it blooms on the morning of Tet, it means prosperity. Put the branch in water and trim it, and the evening before Tet, add a little sugar.

"Leave nothing to chance."

                              Vietnamese Custom

The new year of 1968 was to become the Year of the Monkey, the animal symbolic of intelligence, dexterity and effervescent drive toward progress.

The monkey is also symbolic of cunning.

A half hour into 30 January, the first day of the new Year of the Monkey, enemy forces assaulted Nha Trang. It was the first of seven attacks in the central portion of the country, labeled Viet Cong Military Region 5, beginning one full day before the rest of the Tet attacks. The most widely held theory is that the nationwide offensive was postponed and the commander for that region did not get the word to postpone his attacks for 24 hours.

At dawn on Tuesday, battles raged in Ban Me Thuot, Hoi An, Da Nang, Qui Nhon, Pleiku and Kontum. American and ARVN soldiers fought back with heroic tenacity.

For example, Alpha Troop, 2-1 Cavalry—the "Blackhawks," attached to the U.S. Army 4th Division from the stateside "Hell on Wheels" 2nd Armored Division, was attacked in Kontum by an estimated three enemy battalions. The cavalrymen enacted their rehearsed defensive plan and hung tough...the three battalions were repelled on each of their successive attacks. Alpha Troop was later honored with the Valorous Unit Award for its actions.

At 0945 hours Tuesday, the official Tet truce was canceled by U.S. and South Vietnamese government officials. Reports of the fighting streamed into Westmoreland's headquarters in Saigon, where military men braced for the foreseen attack against the capital city. But Saigon was not ready for war.

Even during the French occupation, Saigon was never attacked. During the American occupation there were sporadic terrorist bombings or sniping incidents, but their city had never been seriously attacked. The enemy forces committed 35 battalions to the attack on Saigon, 11 of which were pitched into the Capital Military District, the most heavily populated area of the city. Most of the enemy were from local force units and did not have far to travel. Their attack was from the north, west and south.

Among the first targets for enemy commandos in Saigon was the United States Embassy. A Viet Cong sapper team entered the embassy compound, killed four guards, and fired rocket propelled grenades into the bolted, four-inch thick teak doors before being silenced.

Thirty-six paratroopers from the 101st Airborne Division stepped onto the embassy roof from hovering helicopters, as Army military policemen and Marines recaptured the compound from the Viet Cong commandos. During the battle for Saigon, the commanding general of the South Vietnamese National Police was filmed and photographed as he executed a captured VC officer. The prisoner, with his hands bound behind his back, was shot in the right temple by a pistol at point blank range.

The fighting also raged fierce in Hue.

A multi-battalion North Vietnamese Army force attack on the Imperial City began at 0330 hours, and 90 minutes later, the gold starred banner of the National Liberation Front flew from the flagpole atop the fortress gate of the Citadel on the northern edge of the River of Perfumes.

These were not black-pajamaed guerrillas, these were hard-core regulars. The bitter street fighting was a first in the war, and enemy troops fighting there surprised officials.

The entire country appeared to have gone insane with this second wave of attacks on 31 January. Teletypes in the Situation Room in the basement of the White House chattered incessantly with reports from Saigon. The phone rang in the Situation Room and an aide answered it; it was President Lyndon B. Johnson calling from the Oval

Office. He wanted to know what the hell was going on.

Giap paced impatiently in his headquarters in Hanoi, waiting for word that the popular uprising he had hoped for in the cities of South Vietnam was taking hold. It was a wasted impatience...the citizen overthrow never materialized.

6

Strategy and The Media

It was becoming clear to General Westmoreland that General Giap's strategy was unfolding as a three-phased attack. First, there were battles along South Vietnam's western borders with Laos and Cambodia. Then came the suicidal raids on the cities. Finally, there would be a Dien Bien Phu-style attack on Khe Sanh. He was sure of it. Westmoreland briefed reporters on February 1st that phase two of the communist offensive was, "about to run out of steam." He predicted the North Vietnamese violation of the Tet truce would fail.

THE MEDIA

Vietnam was the first televised war for Americans and the world. Tet was the first television superbattle. It had the unprecedented power to instantly sway public opinion without regard to perspective.

The high drama and low national understanding of Vietnam created a natural vacuum for journalists to fill. The images of the Tet offensive raced from the battlefield to dinner-time living rooms halfway around the world, with no balance or reasoned judgment.

The credibility that Westmoreland's ramrod straight persona had established with the American public three months prior had turned black. In November 1967, he had publicly predicted success in South Vietnam, "lies within our grasp." The parade of Tet images flickering across American television sets proclaimed that the winter confidence for victory in Southeast Asia was without foundation.

American military men bemoaned the coverage of Tet. They believed the sense of panic felt at home was out of proportion to the actual situation. "We're winning," they argued. Militarily speaking, they were right.

But the North Vietnamese won something more precious than battles...they won the support of American public outcry against the war.

One of the devices that defeated the French in Indochina was Giap's insistence the war must be won by popular discontent in the enemy's own country. The North Vietnamese helped to create sensational headlines during Tet which dented the armor of American resolve back home. Television and newspaper reports fueled the angry cries of dissidents on American soil.

The media portrayed the communists as having taken the initiative in the war. Most Americans at home were unprepared for this stunning show of determination. Their first reaction was a jump in support of the war, but this wave of patriotism crumbled quickly as the public experienced via television airwaves, among other things, the murder of the Viet Cong officer by the chief of the South Vietnamese National Police, who acted as a one-man judge, jury and executioner. Summaries by officials on actual battlefield tallies were not believed in lieu of what the people saw. The overriding emotion was that the war in Vietnam was a stalemate and a mistake.

And the third phase of Giap's purported three-pronged attack had not yet occurred.

7

The Siege of Khe Sanh

The new year 1968 was barely more than two days old when Marines on the western perimeter of the Khe Sanh combat base tensed as a sentry dog alerted them to the sight of six Orientals outside the defensive wire. They were dressed in Marine battle dress uniforms and stood in a group, apparently studying the base defenses.

A Marine guard hollered at the group and when they hesitated to answer too long, five of the six died in a hail of rifle fire. The sole survivor grabbed the group's map case and limped into the jungle.

Intelligence experts determined the dead men to be NVA officers from a regimental staff on a personal reconnaissance of the Marine base; a fatal undertaking which signaled a definite assault on the U.S. forces at Khe Sanh.

The enemy situation map in the command bunker was quickly updated. Sources reported 2 regiments of the NVA 325C Division about 15 miles to the northwest of Khe Sanh, 2 regiments of the 320th Division about 15 miles to the northeast, and the 304th Division across the border inside Laos.

The Americans filled in the details. The 325C was a veteran of the Hill Fights and the 304th carried battle streamers from Dien Bien Phu. The approximately 20,000 men of these two divisions were buttressed by the NVA 68th and 164th Artillery Regiments, and possibly some armored columns. By the end of the first week in January, General Westmoreland had ordered all information gathering sources to concentrate on the jungled valleys around Khe Sanh...and the fate of the combat base loomed clearer.

Marines on the perimeter readied for the onslaught. One night, the empty C-ration tin cans hooked on the defensive wire on the western edge of the base jingled and caught the attention of a Marine Corps private. He stared open-mouthed through his Starlight scope—a night vision device which uses available light from the celestial bodies to illuminate the field of sight, as one tiger, a descendant of survivors of the emperor's hunts, "at least nine feet long," leaped the eight-foot tall concertina wire barrier.

The cat foraged around "in the trash pits for a while," and then jumped the wire again "as calmly as a tomcat over a frontyard picket fence" and melted back into the jungle.

A false alarm, but the Marines still braced themselves. The enemy, presumably poised to strike, did not come.

Westmoreland revealed his fire plan to Colonel David Lownds on 6 January, to provide support to the base and the American-held hills beyond. The fire plan was codenamed, "Niagra," for the image of cascading bombs from the skies. All Lownds, the combat base commander, had to do was send a radio message to the airplanes circling the skies over Khe Sanh to undam the torrent.

On 16 January, Lownds had received the 1,000 man 2nd Battalion of his regiment at Khe Sanh. He sent them to Hill 558, where they perched, over the Rao Quan River Valley and blocked the approach to Khe Sanh. From that position, they could also pour fire onto the enemy assaulting Hill 861.

It was the first time since Iwo Jima in the Second World War that the entire regiment had operated together in combat. Iwo Jima had special significance for Lownds. He had earned the Purple Heart on the island for wounds suffered in combat as a young infantryman.

Lownds also reinforced the 300 infantrymen of India Company on Hill 881 South with another 100 riflemen. Reinforcements or not, the now 400 Marines of India company knew they would have to fight if overrun; overland relief from the combat base was not possible.

The same sense of dread descended on the 200 men of Kilo Company on Hill 861, and also on the platoon on Hill 950 guarding the radio antennas that electronically linked the combat base with Dong Ha.

Additional fire support was fit into the defensive plan when the big 175s at Camp Carroll and the Rockpile were ordered to aim west toward Khe Sanh.

In all, Lownds had fire support from 46 artillery pieces of all calibers, five 90-millimeter tanks and 92 single, or Ontos, mounted 106-millimeter recoilless rifles. The Ontos is a squat, lightly-armored, tracked vehicle boasting six 106s each. It was originally designed as a tank killer, but now armed with flechette rounds, thousands of tiny winged darts could pepper the enemy with instant death. It became an impressive supporter of the infantry.

And Lownds had "Niagra".

He breathed easier, but it was a brief respite.

Enemy small arms fire and rocket-propelled grenades slammed into the men of India Company on patrol between Hills 881 South and 881 North before noon on 20 January.

One platoon of Marines flanked a dug-in enemy position like "a page out of the life of Chesty Puller." The Leathernecks of India Company continued their counterattack with a savage fervor and supporting fire from the howitzers on Hill 881 South and the combat base. Fighter bombers ignited the underbrush with fiery napalm as 500-pound bombs released from Marine jets literally blew the tops off the small hills housing well-fortified enemy positions. The back of the enemy ambush was broken.

Radio reports streaked to the combat base where Marines tensed for the offensive they'd waited for, when a white flag was seen waving outside the wire on the eastern edge of the airstrip. NVA First Lieutenant La Than Tonc had surrendered.

Tonc was rushed to the intelligence bunker where he introduced himself as an anti-aircraft company commander. He had fought for 14 years, he explained, and was passed over for promotion. He had had enough of the war.

Tonc detailed the plans of an upcoming attack on the Khe Sanh combat base. He detailed plans of forthcoming attacks on Dong Ha and Quang Tri. He detailed plans of the imminent communist offensive that would encompass all of I Corps.

The information matched reports the intelligence sources had gathered. Lownds believed Tonc, that the enemy would attack Hill

861 in a few hours as a preface to the offensive. Lownds had nothing to lose by believing. Kilo Company was radioed and readied.

Shortly after midnight on the 21st, the enemy attacked as planned.

A bitter fight ensued, but the American-held hilltops nearby were quiet. The eighteen 105s and six 155s of the combat base pounded the enemy soldiers as they swarmed near the crest of Hill 861. Spirited gunners and "ammo humpers" from one mortar pit on the hill bellowed out hearty stanzas of the Marine Corps Hymn as they fired on the charging NVA infantry. Exchanges of short range rifle fire and vicious hand-to-hand combat finally threw the enemy from the crown in this deadly version of King-of-the-Hill.

Minutes after the victory, near first light, with thick fog cutting visibility down to 30 meters, the combat base came under brutal rocket and artillery attack. The first of the rockets pierced the ammo dump, which ignited into tremendous explosion after explosion. The military term for a series of connected detonations is "sympathetic." There was nothing sympathetic about this.

Clouds of tear gas from Marine supplies drifted fog-thick across the base, as fires erupted blast-furnace hot. The Marines donned protective masks, which were practically useless in the concentrated gas clouds, and braced for an assault.

The small contingent of Marines, Regional Force soldiers and Army advisors commanded by U.S. Army Captain Bruce Clarke in Khe Sanh Village watched the sky above the combat base plateau glow in the light of explosions; then steeled themselves as NVA infantry assaulted the western end of the town.

More than 1,000 rounds of artillery from the base and a relay of sorties pushed the attackers back again.

On 22 January, Lownds decided to evacuate his Marines from the village while able to do so, after the initial attack failed and the NVA withdrew. The Special Forces at Lang Vei received the news and offered the recently arrived MIKE Force company to the Marines, to fortify the village compound. The enemy had been thrown back twice, they argued, and the 196-man mercenary force could help hold the village, which was their supply link to the combat base.

The Marines said no. Leathernecks in the village compound were whisked to the combat base by helicopters. It was recommended to

Clarke to leave the compound as well. The Regional Force company and U.S. Army advisors would have to walk to the combat base.

By nightfall, the U.S. advisory compound in Khe Sanh Village was abandoned.

First Lieutenant Paul R. Longgrear and a platoon of his MIKEs slipped into the western perimeter of the town near dusk. Evening mists clung to the narrow village streets and bathed the battle-pocked hootches in an otherworldliness. Enemy soldiers slept fitfully by the roadside fires they built to heat their dinners. Longgrear led his patrol carefully back toward the western edge of the town, and then scurried home.

He reported to Captain Frank Willoughby the results of his reconnaissance. The Marines no longer held the village, nor did the advisors, and Lang Vei now dangled like an apple on a twig weakened by a greenstick fracture. The one physical link between the combat base and the camp had dissolved. They were on their own.

OPPOSITION AT HOME

Self-appointed experts in the United States, critical of our involvement in Southeast Asia, learned of the latest fighting and lashed out in opposition to the manning of the Khe Sanh combat base. They said enemy forces could effectively keep the reinforced Marine regiment penned up while their comrades could skirt the perimeter of the base to head east on Highway 9 unopposed.

Or, that the enemy could overrun Khe Sanh. Giap was supposed to be the Asian Napoleon, they argued, who had handed the French their defeat on the battlefield.

These critical Americans pointed out that the Marines could not block NVA infiltration into Quang Tri Province. They believed the base could easily become surrounded by the enemy. They feared an American Dien Bien Phu.

Westmoreland had thought the same thing, but not out of fatalism. He thought about Dien Bien Phu, studied Dien Bien Phu and then prepared his forces in case Giap attempted to repeat history. He wanted Giap to try. He wanted Khe Sanh to lure thousands of enemy soldiers to their deaths around that combat base. He wanted a nose-to-nose confrontation in conventional warfare. Dien Bien Phu was to represent nothing more than lessons learned for the Americans, he chided his staff, and not some overwhelming will that the enemy could force on U.S. troops at their whim.

Westmoreland decided the Marines would stay at Khe Sanh.

NUCLEAR WEAPONS

On 2 February, President Lyndon B. Johnson asked Westmoreland about the possibility of using nuclear weapons at Khe Sanh.

"We should be prepared to introduce weapons of greater effectiveness," Westmoreland said as he briefed General Earle G. Wheeler, chairman of the Joint Chiefs of Staff. "Under such circumstances (massed enemy infantry attacks), I visualize that either tactical nuclear weapons or chemical agents would be active candidates for deployment. Because the region (is) virtually uninhabited, civilian casualties would be minimal."

News of the discussions on the possible employment of nuclear weapons in Vietnam splashed the front pages of newspapers a week later. The public revelation forced Johnson administration officials to declare that the Joint Chiefs neither recommended nor requested the use of nuclear weapons. Wheeler called Westmoreland and told him to stop planning for their use.

Westmoreland thought it was a mistake, but he complied.

Besides, he wasn't nearly out of aces for Khe Sanh. He had recently granted the Marines at the combat base the capability and authority to use COFRAM, a new "butterfly type" artillery shell which fragmented into slivers of metal that would shred any charging enemy.

Aerial resupply by parachute and Low Altitude Parachute Extraction was ready.

"Niagra" was ready.

In an unprecedented event, the Joint Chiefs of Staff signed a written promise to President Johnson that Khe Sanh could successfully be held.

There would be no damned Dien Bien Phu in Westmoreland's command.

Part II

8

Callsign, "Jacksonville"

U.S. Marine Corps Staff Sergeant Thomas J. "Jim" Gagnon shuffled through the shrouds of afternoon fog clinging to the Khe Sanh Combat Base and sat down to write a letter on a red, dust-covered pile of sand bags near the Fire Direction Center (FDC) bunker.

Awakening like this kept things in a dream-like state; sleep was never sound in this first week of the siege. Rather, it was like an exhausted, one-eye-open rest. Gagnon tried to wipe the dust from his lap, which served as a desk from which to write his parents in New Hampshire. But the dust was everywhere and permeated the Marines at the combat base to the pore. He gave up trying to clean his fatigue pants and scrawled "6 Feb" on his note pad.

Gagnon was a man of few words, spoken or written. He almost never wrote his parents, but they were caring for his children while he was in Vietnam and lately he could not shake this feeling of impending doom. He felt he was going to die at Khe Sanh. He felt compelled to write his family one last time.

"If it ain't the incoming, it's the outgoing...if it ain't the outgoing it's the incoming," a beleaguered Marine muttered to himself in sheer frustration as he passed Gagnon in a crouched half-run, moving to seek cover in a nearby bunker. Gagnon grinned a knowing half-smile and a split second later, heard the enemy incoming artillery, sounding like small animals scurrying through dry leaves as it passed overhead.

USMC Staff Sergeant Tom Gagnon relaxes in a Fire Direction Center in 1968. Gagnon was the artillery operations chief at Khe Sanh who fired the Marine guns in defense of the Lang Vei camp during the 1968 tank battle.

Photo courtesy of Tom Gagnon

The shells were being lobbed from Co Roc Mountain, an impregnable natural fortress ten kilometers west of the combat base, just over the border into Laos. The shells tore into the center of the base with an ear shattering roar, as they had been doing daily for the past couple of weeks, steadily wearing the Marines down. Gagnon, too, sought cover.

U.S. military historians scoffed at the idea that the incoming artillery and rocket fire at Khe Sanh was brutal. They pointed to battles in the Second World War where artillery duels really were brutal in terms of the number of rounds expended.

At Khe Sanh, it wasn't the number of shells that pounded the base so much as it was their persistence. Hour after hour of restless sleep was pocked by just enough of a reminder that the guns on Co Roc were there—and would never be silenced throughout the siege.

The assignment at Khe Sanh was during the latter part of Gagnon's second tour in Vietnam. He first landed at Da Nang in 1965 with the first wave of Marine combat troops, sent to secure the airfield near that port city. When he returned in 1967, he was surprised to find Da Nang now housed, in addition to the airfield, a large rear area combat base; headquarters for the 5th Special Forces Group (ABN), which was responsible for all operations in I—pronounced, EYE Corps; and a sprawling rest and recreation center.

Artillery was Gagnon's specialty. His combat smarts were honed from his first tour of flying the one-oh-five (105 millimeter) Howitzer guns strapped beneath the bellies of the CH-46 helicopters into the jungle; "Indian country," as the Marines called it. The survivability of the 6,000 Marines at Khe Sanh meant relying on the artillery, which responded daily to the fury of the 122-millimeter rockets and the 130- and 152-millimeter Soviet-made shells showering in from Co Roc and from south of the French fort.

Khe Sanh was being referred to in higher circles as, "Westmoreland's Dien Bien Phu," and the 304th carried battle streamers from that historic fight with the French. Marines on the perimeter had never heard of Dien Bien Phu; of the defeat of the French forces on the valley floor during the battle, whose sights and sounds gave Bernard Fall the title of his book, *Hell In A Very Small Place*. They only waited for the enemy.

102

This aerial view of Highway 9 from the Khe Sanh Combat Base to the Lang Vei camp shows some of the hilly terrain which limited the use of enemy tanks in the area in 1968.

Photo courtesy of Tom Gagnon

Gagnon's unit, the 1st Battalion, 13th Field Artillery Regiment (1/13) sent a Forward Observer (FO) to the Special Forces camp at Lang Vei in January, to pre-plan supporting fires. Green Berets gave the FO some chow and smoked and joked with him a while, grateful for any help the Marines could give them.

Dangling beyond the edge of the protective artillery umbrella of the big 175-millimeter Army guns at Camp J.J. Carroll to the east, the Special Forces needed the Marines. Whatever animosity was felt between the two combat organizations at higher levels did not seem to drift down to the troops in the field.

The FO plotted potential target areas on his map to take back to Khe Sanh, so the Marine guns could train their fury on the Lang Vei landscape. "If you need us, our callsign's, 'Jacksonville,'" he said to the Green Berets before he scurried aboard the helicopter that would whisk him back to the combat base.

* * *

Incoming artillery rounds sound a lot like outgoing ones to the untrained ear, except for the explosion. By now, Gagnon could not only distinguish between the two sounds, but could "guesstimate" where the incoming rounds were going to impact.

At first he would chuckle when newly arrived Marines at Khe Sanh would scramble for cover as U.S. guns thundered out replies to NVA artillery, confusing the sounds with incoming rounds. Then, one night a bunker was hit that housed nearly thirty replacements…Marines who had arrived at Khe Sanh…who had not yet inprocessed. An enemy shell landed squarely on top of the sand bagged shelter and killed all of the new Marines. It wasn't funny anymore.

Gagnon hunkered down in the FDC bunker as enemy shells pounded the base. He put off writing his parents for now, but the feeling of impending doom would grow deeper and blacker. Shortly, he would go on night shift as the operations chief of the artillery center; the 1/13th Field Artillery defending Khe Sanh and the Special Forces camp at Lang Vei.

9

Longgrear's "Yards"

The only Montagnard combat units that did not have Vietnamese leaders were the Mobile Strike—MIKE—Forces. These MIKEs differed from the Civilian Irregular Defense Groups on two counts: they did not fight in the areas in which they lived, like the CIDG did, and they were mercenaries with special training. The MIKEs were airborne qualified and their American leaders paid them for the weapons they collected from the victims of their attacks. American Green Berets commanded the MIKE units and the Montagnard soldiers held subordinate leadership positions.

The MIKEs sent to Lang Vei in December 1967 were from the Hre tribe near Ban Me Thuot. The American commander of the MIKE company, U.S. Army First Lieutenant Paul Longgrear, inherited the unit weeks before as the executive officer, and then assumed command.

Longgrear was given the task of getting the company combat ready. The Hre soldiers in this particular company had earned a reputation for running in battle, attributed to poor leadership since they were normally regarded as tough troops.

The Hres did not lack combat experience. One of Longgrear's Hre platoon leaders was a middle-aged Montagnard named, "Blo," who was commissioned in the French Army and who had a son in his platoon. Blo's platoon sergeant, "Jang," was a combat veteran and held two American combat awards. Even Longgrear's interpreter was seasoned. The interpreter, a 16-year-old part-Hre, part-French

1LT Paul R. Longgrear, front, poses with members of his US Army Special Forces "A" team during a public display of Green Berets in the United States in 1967. Long-grear later commanded the MIKE Force at Lang Vei during the 1968 tank battle and was trapped in the command bunker until the breakout during the afternoon of 7 February 1968.

Soldiers from the MIKE force company at the Lang Vei Special Forces camp conduct a tactical road march west on Highway 9 as they leave their observation point—actually a mini-camp a half-mile west of the Lang Vei compound—in search of the enemy in January 1968.

Photo courtesy of
Paul R. Longgrear

Montagnard named, "Blue," who had red hair, enjoyed a tough reputation as a young man who loved to knife fight.

Longgrear and his four American Special Forces soldiers leading the company put the unit out on patrol to make contact with light enemy forces, practice their fighting skills, and bolster their sagging confidence. The training was effective in a short time and Longgrear's unit was sent north to Lang Vei to strengthen the CIDG camp.

The camp commander, Captain Frank Willoughby, who was a Special Forces school classmate of Longgrear's, did not allow the Hre to mingle with his Bru soldiers. The Bru, who populated the camp and nearby Lang Vei and other villages, were fighting on the land on which they lived; the Hre were just visitors. Willoughby put the Hre company on an "Observation Post" a half mile to the west of the camp on Highway 9. An Observation Post (OP) in military parlance is a point of terrain with a handful of men occupying it, whose job is to provide early warning to the bulk of the unit should an attack be detected. Lang Vei had a 196-man OP.

The Hre felt snubbed. Contact with the enemy was light during the latter part of December and Longgrear had to intervene more than once when his MIKE troops threatened to go over to the Bru camp and "shoot them up." The segregation was only part of it. Longgrear acknowledged that his Hres, whom he affectionately referred to as his "Yards," probably stirred up trouble with the Bru by offering to buy their women. The problem was the MIKEs were being worked too hard.

The MIKEs were sent out on continuous patrols to determine enemy troop locations and strengths. Patrolling was second nature to the Hres. They had been part of a larger, experimental project before joining Lang Vei known as the "Mobile Guerrilla Force" (MGF). Nothing like "enemy lines" existed in Vietnam, but there were NVA sanctuaries in Laos, Cambodia, North Vietnam, and South Vietnam that were solely enemy territory. The MGF was conceived as a project to operate in those suspected sanctuaries, to harass enemy communications lines, and to occupy the efforts of NVA units moving south.

The MIKE Force patrols at Lang Vei were not permitted to cross the Sepone River into Laos unless they were in "hot pursuit" of the enemy. Two MIKE platoon leaders, Sergeant First Class Harvey

Soldiers from the MIKE force company reinforcing the Lang Vei Special Forces "A" camp cross the Sepone River and patrol into Laos. With the camp so close to enemy sanctuaries, patrols sought to confirm rumors of enemy tanks barely a mile from their camp in January 1968.

Photo courtesy of Paul R. Longgrear

Brande and Sergeant John Early, would lead their patrols to the river, call the camp on the radio stating they were pursuing a fleeing enemy (and fire off a few M16 rounds for effect), and then cross into Laos.

On one such patrol, the two platoons "located an empty tank park a few kilometers across the river, which contained fresh impressions of tracked vehicles." The patrol was ambushed and fought its way back across the river to Lang Vei. Their radio reports of the tank park were dismissed by Marines at Khe Sanh who felt they were "exaggerated or false."

They were told by the Marines that they were "trying to make themselves look good, the NVA doesn't have tanks." Perhaps the reports were discounted because the ruse to cross the river was suspected, and maybe the MIKEs had cried "Wolf" once too often. But there were other incidents where the Marines refused to believe.

On one occasion, a patrol discovered elephants near the border and it was surmised they were used to pack NVA mortars. Marines at Da Nang refused to believe. One Special Forces NCO reportedly flew over the Marine command bunker in Da Nang and dropped elephant feces from the helicopter onto the bunker, while hollering over the radio, "Believe this!"

Longgrear's relationship with his fellow Green Berets on the "A" team was a "real love-hate affair." He complained to Willoughby that his MIKEs were doing too much patrolling and the "A" team and CIDG were not doing enough.

Willoughby and Longgrear had served in the same battalion at the Fort Benning (Georgia) Infantry Center prior to going to the Special Forces training group together. They sought a compromise and decided each patrol would be assigned an American from the "A" team and one from the MIKE Force, since all patrols had to have two Americans with it.

On the night of 6 February 1968, Sergeant First Class Kenneth Hanna, from A-101, accompanied Sergeant First Class Charles Lindewald and his MIKE Force platoon out to the OP.

CHARLIE WAS FROM LA PORTE, IND.

10

Countdown to The Battle

21 January—The Village

The squad of U.S. Marines and U.S. Army advisors, commanded by U.S. Army Captain Bruce B.G. Clarke, together with their Regional Force/Popular Force Company of ARVN, repelled two NVA attacks against the advisory compound in Khe Sanh Village.

The advisory group had been in the village since the accidental bombing of Montagnards at nearby Lang Vei Village in January 1967 practically destroyed relations between the Americans and the Bru. The village, for a time, offered a brief respite to Marines at the combat base. An enterprising restauranteur in Khe Sanh Village offered noodle dishes to soldiers who had grown weary of combat rations, and the Americans called his place, "Howard Johnson's." The village also housed, in addition to the Bru, American missionaries and French plantation owners. Many Americans believed the French and the police chief were paying the NVA and VC "protection" money, but felt sorry for these people caught in the middle of the war and patronized the town whenever they could.

Now the village was lost.

Clarke radioed the Khe Sanh Combat Base and requested the previously ordered relief force of Marines on standby be sent to help reinforce the compound. The Marine company reached Hill 471, looked down at the village advisory compound, and seeing it was surrounded, radioed Clarke that they were returning to the combat base.

Despite the victorious efforts of the contingent of troops in the compound, the Marine headquarters in Quang Tri ordered Colonel David Lownds to retrieve his Marines from Khe Sanh Village back to the combat base. The Special Forces soldiers at Lang Vei offered the Marines their newly arrived company of MIKE Force troops, but the Marines declined the offer to reinforce the village.

Helicopters were sent to evacuate the Marines; the Americans and the Regional Force/Popular Force company had to walk the three kilometers to the combat base. Many hid their uniforms and weapons beneath borrowed Vietnamese pajamas to avoid enemy detection. When they arrived at the combat base, the Americans were housed in the SOG compound, FOB-3, on the southwestern edge of the combat base.

Later that afternoon, an FOB-3/advisor conducted a heliborne raid back into the Khe Sanh Village compound and brought out the more than 150 remaining weapons captured following the NVA attack.

The South Vietnamese Regional Force/Popular Force company that had to walk from the village to the combat base was turned away at the Khe Sanh Combat Base wire; the Marines would not allow indigenous troops inside their defenses.

22 January—Tanks in Laos

Reconnaissance airplanes and fighter bombers circled the fog-choked skies over the Khe Sanh Combat Base. Aerial communications laboratories processed electronic information sent in by the acoustic and seismic sensors strewn in the valleys west of the combat base, when a cry for help was received on a tactical radio frequency. The request for assistance came from a Laotian unit some 12 miles west of the combat base, just inside Laos.

The Laotian Army unit reported it was being overrun by NVA infantry and the attack was led by tanks. A Forward Air Controller (FAC), and two bomb-laden fighter planes went to their aid in the hopes of getting a shot at the first wholesale appearance of enemy armor in the war. Million-candle-power flares dropped from the planes failed to illuminate the tanks and were swallowed in the milky mists. Their radios picked up the last cries for help from the ground they could not see and then went dead. The planes returned to South Vietnam before they could get a shot at the tanks.

24 January—The Elephant Battalion Walks In

The members of the 33rd Royal Laotian Elephant Battalion and their families straggled east on Highway 9 from Laos. They are stopped and disarmed by the MIKE Force a half-mile west of the Special Forces Camp at Lang Vei. The Lao battalion commander, a lieutenant colonel, conferred with "A" team members and Captain Frank Willoughby, the team commander. The Lao colonel reported that tanks overran his unit in Laos two days before and that there were enemy tanks. The lack of casualties and their seemingly unfired weapons caused the Green Berets to discount the claim.

Even so, Willoughby ordered 100 light anti-tank weapons (LAWs) for the camp. The Lao battalion was sent to Old Lang Vei a half-mile to the west, the site of the 1967 battle when the Green Beret camp was overrun. A contingent of six Special Forces soldiers arrived the next day with barrier materials, ammunition, food, and medical supplies to assist the Laotians.

30 January—The Hoi Chanh and Other Intelligence

A North Vietnamese Army private named, Luong Dinh Du surrendered to the Green Berets at Lang Vei. He stumbled from the brush, walked past the Bru guards sleeping at the gate, and shocked the Special Forces soldiers when he approached them in the teamhouse. He was hastily interrogated and the information he gave the Green Berets was sketchy at best. He did tell them that an attack was planned for their camp, but he did not know when.

Later, in the hands of skilled Marine interrogators, Du revealed that he had heard the unmistakable clanking of tanks with his unit

A column of 220 refugees, soldiers and family members of the 33d Royal Laotian Elephant Battalion, rest along Highway 9 outside the US Army Special Forces camp at Lang Vei on 24 January 1968. The Lao battalion commander told the Green Berets that NVA tanks overran his unit two days prior in Laos.

Photo courtesy of Paul R. Longgrear

as they moved south along the Ho Chi Minh Trail, although he had not personally seen the vehicles.

Later on the 30th, an American from the Lang Vei camp was taken prisoner by the North Vietnamese. U.S. Army Staff Sergeant John Young had been in Vietnam for about a month and served with the Special Forces "C" team in Da Nang. He was sent to Lang Vei with the Green Berets to take care of the Laotians and had been there only a couple of days when Willoughby sent him on patrol with some Laotian soldiers to reconnoiter a village to the northeast of Lang Vei. The patrol walked east and then north on Highway 9. When the soldiers left the road to move cross country, they came under fire. Young returned fire, but his Laotians scattered and he was led away as prisoner of the North Vietnamese Army.

Another patrol that same day from Lang Vei discovered a crossing site on the Sepone River, built into a stream bed so vehicles could pass undetected from Laos into South Vietnam.

Special Forces troops at Lang Vei monitored the radio for reports of fighting in the central part of the country. The Tet Offensive had begun.

31 January—Captain Willoughby Rethinks Strategy

A patrol proceeded cautiously from Lang Vei toward Khe Sanh Village. When the fog suddenly parted, the MIKE Force troops opened fire on an estimated battalion of NVA soldiers camped near the village. Small arms fire, machine gun fire, and coordinated airstrikes bombarded the surprised enemy troops, and resulted in 54 NVA killed and 30 weapons captured.

The increased pressure on the camp caused Willoughby to rethink his strategy. He decided to pull two-thirds of the MIKE Force on the observation point into the camp and he fit them into the camp's defenses like pieces in a now-completed puzzle. One platoon of the MIKE Force would occupy the OP at night to provide early warning and initial engagement of the enemy, who might come from Laos on Highway 9.

The Green Berets continued to monitor radio reports of fighting, which now engulfed South Vietnam. The Tet Offensive by the enemy

was now in full force throughout the rest of the country. The Special
Forces at Lang Vei and Marines at the Khe Sanh combat base peered
into the thick night fog and tensed for the assault they knew would
come.

But for now the night was quiet.

6 February—Incoming; the NVA Prepare

U.S. Army Lieutenant Colonel Daniel Schungel flew into the Lang
Vei camp in the afternoon. Schungel, commander of the Special Forces
"C" team in Da Nang, replaced his executive officer, Major Hoadley,
as the field grade officer on site. Schungel decided to keep a higher
ranking military official than Willoughby at Lang Vei to soothe the
feelings of the Lao battalion commander at the old camp, and now
it was his turn. The third field grade officer in Special Forces I Corps
was Major Adam Husar, commander of the MIKE Force battalion
at Da Nang and Longgrear's boss. Husar was to replace Schungel
at Lang Vei on 7 February.

Lieutenant Bailey departed the camp to Da Nang to take care of
personal business; he was to report back in a couple of days. As a
contingency in case the camp was attacked, he was to man a
106-millimeter recoilless rifle, one of the camp's two such rifles, facing
west on Highway 9. A replacement was not designated.

The Lang Vei camp had experienced frequent mortar and artillery
barrages since the first part of February, fire which coincided with
the landing of resupply helicopters. Helicopter crewmen were becoming adept at quickly kicking out the supply bundles for the camp as
the aircraft made a low level approach; they knew the enemy artillery
would quickly follow.

Three mortar rounds impacted inside the camp that morning, and
4.2-inch mortar fire was employed at the suspected enemy mortar
sites. Shortly before 1900 hours, an estimated 30 to 40 rounds screamed
into the camp from Co Roc Mountain. Two soldiers were wounded
and two bunkers were damaged in the afternoon assault.

Soldiers at Lang Vei employed counterbattery fire again and all firing
ceased about 1900 hours.

Longgrear sent one of his MIKE platoons to man the OP. Accompanying the Hres were Sergeant First Class Charles Lindewald, one of his platoon leaders, and Sergeant First Class Kenneth Hanna from the "A" team. The OP force hardly left the camp's gate when Longgrear heard rifle fire and saw his platoon scurrying back into the camp. Schungel heard the ruckus and wanted to know what the hell was going on.

"What happened?" Longgrear demanded. "I don't know, Sir," one of the sergeants explained. "They (the Hres) said they saw something and got spooked."

"Many...many VC," the Montagnards said in agreement with the American.

Longgrear said they had to man the OP for the night. The Hres said no. Schungel was furious.

Longgrear explained to his Montagnards that they were causing him to lose face with his commander, they were causing the American sergeants with them to look like cowards. No, the Montagnards protested, they were not cowards. Well, Longgrear said, then you have to man the OP. Okay, they said, we'll go.

With the OP finally in place, Schungel took the VNSF commander, Lieutenant Quan, and the VNSF operations officer, Lieutenant Quy, on an inspection of the camp perimeter at last light, approximately 2000 hours. The soldiers, with the exception of those on watch, turned in.

Soldiers at the Company 104 perimeter reported hearing engine noises from the vicinity of Lang Troai Road to the south of the camp. The MIKEs on the OP also reported engine noises from the west along Highway 9. Three trip flares ignited near the OP and the MIKEs began firing. The CIDG, gripped by the tension, also began firing. There was no return fire and the camp became quiet. The fog was settling in thick white sheets, which added to the spookiness of the already tense camp.

A trip flare burst into its brilliant white light near the Company 104 perimeter at 2240 hours, and the CIDG fired once more into the night. The weapons fire died away after a few minutes.

Staff Sergeant John Young was being held by the North Vietnamese about three kilometers west of the Lang Vei camp. In the week he'd been held prisoner, he was interrogated by his captors about the defenses of the camp. Young insisted he wasn't in the camp long enough to know its defenses. The North Vietnamese took a Lao prisoner and shot him in the head at point blank range.

They asked Young again. He insisted that he didn't know. The North Vietnamese killed another Lao prisoner.

Finally, he was shown a regular 1:50,000 army map on which U.S. positions at Khe Sanh and Lang Vei were marked in detail. His captors showed him a dozen five-by-seven photographs taken with a 35-mm telephoto lens of Lang Vei's mortar pits, gun positions, and teamhouse. Young felt they had been planning an assault on Lang Vei for quite some time.

The North Vietnamese pointed at the pictures and asked Young to identify the obvious, an attempt to seek verification of what they already knew.

Young pointed at the helicopter landing pad and said, "Highway 9 runs through here and the Vietnamese and Americans are over here at the new camp."

He was asked how many men were in the camp and the locations of specific firing positions. Young said he didn't know. His captor pointed a pistol at Young's eyes, and he felt as though he would be killed like the two Lao prisoners had been moments before.

Young insisted he didn't know. He was allowed to live.

On 6 February, an unusually cheerful interrogator approached Young and asked him, "Would you like to watch us overrun Lang Vei tonight?"

7 February—The Attack Begins

Forty-two minutes after midnight, Sergeant Nickolas Fragos' attention was focused on the defensive wire near Company 104. He watched from his position atop the command bunker as two enemy soldiers began to calmly cut the defensive wire. There were two tanks behind them; the tank commanders appeared "almost casual" in their cupolas. The whole scene was bathed in the eerie, flickering green light of a trip flare that announced their arrival.

"Why don't they just roll over the wire?" Fragos wondered to himself. CIDG soldiers from Company 104 saw the enemy too, hesitated for a moment, and then mowed down the two dismounted enemy soldiers in a hail of gunfire. The tanks buttoned up and bulled over the perimeter fence as Fragos hollered into his radio handset, "We have tanks in the wire!"

American Green Berets at Lang Vei

Team A-101

Captain Frank Willoughby, team commander
First Lieutenant Miles R. Wilkins, team executive officer
First Lieutenant Bailey (left Lang Vei on 6 February 1968,
    for two days on personal business in Da Nang)
Sergeant First Class William T. Craig, team sergeant
Sergeant First Class James Holt, medic
Sergeant First Class Kenneth Hanna, weapons specialist
Staff Sergeant Dennis L. Thompson, radio operator
Staff Sergeant Peter Tiroch, intelligence specialist
Staff Sergeant Emmanuel E. Phillips, radio operator
Staff Sergeant Arthur Brooks, weapons specialist
Sergeant Nickolas Fragos, medic
Sergeant Dan Phillips, demolitions specialist
Specialist Four William G. McMurray, radio operator
Specialist Four Franklin H. Dooms, radio operator

MIKE Force

First Lieutenant Paul R. Longgrear, company commander
Sergeant First Class Earl Burke, platoon leader
Sergeant First Class Charles Lindewald, platoon leader
Sergeant First Class Harvey G. Brande, platoon leader
Sergeant John Early, platoon leader
Specialist Four James L. "Wes" Moreland, medic

Assistance Team at Old Lang Vei

Lieutenant Colonel Daniel F. Schungel, "C" team commander
    from Da Nang
First Lieutenant Thomas E. Todd, engineer
Sergeant First Class Eugene Ashley, Jr., medic

Staff Sergeant John Young (captured by the North Vietnamese Army
near Khe Sanh Village during a patrol on 30 January, 1968)
Sergeant Richard H. Allen, medic
Specialist Four Joel Johnson, medic

11

The Battle of Lang Vei

First Lieutenant Paul Longgrear was exhausted. Tension at the camp, present for weeks, was heightened by the Hre refusal to man the OP. After they finally left the camp for the OP site, Longgrear settled down for the night at the camp's southeastern 81-millimeter mortar pit with one of his platoon leaders, Sergeant John Early. Sporadic firing by Montagnards on the perimeter, spooked by eerie fog-shrouded shadows and igniting trip flares, increased the tension.

Then came the cry, "We have tanks in the wire!" over the radio. There was a pause.

"Say what?" came the surprised reply from the command bunker.

Sergeant Nick Fragos hardly heard this call for confirmation amid the cracks and pops of M-16s and AK-47s at close range. "Jesus Christ," he shouted into the radio handset, "I've got five tanks and a couple of hundred gooks on top of me! They're all over the fucking place! Get me some illumination!"

Longgrear, Early, and Staff Sergeant Dennis L. Thompson fired some illumination rounds from the 81, and then picked up LAWs. They peered into the darkness of the south perimeter where red and green tracers criss-crossed in the milky blackness.

Longgrear saw a tank bulling its way into the inner perimeter toward his mortar pit. He armed the anti-tank weapon and depressed the rubber trigger mechanism. Nothing happened.

Early handed him another. He armed the second one and fired it.

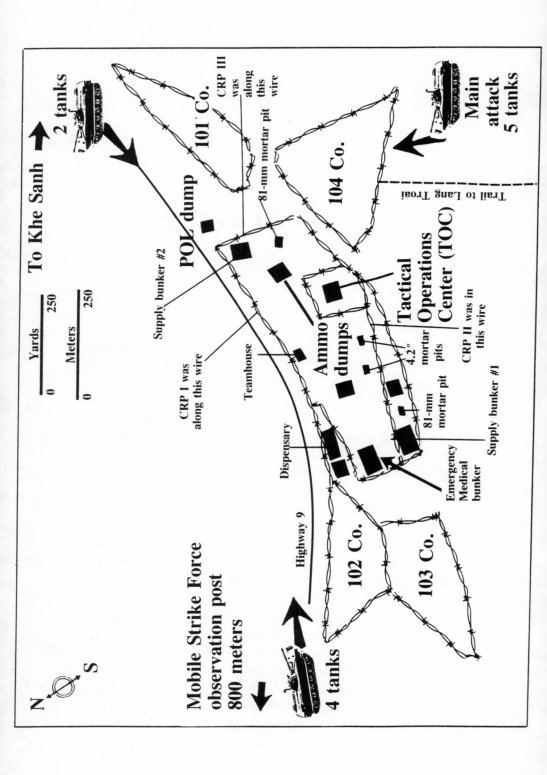

Nothing happened.

Thompson handed him another. Longgrear armed it and squeezed the trigger. Nothing. He armed it again and fired. The warhead jumped from the tube with a *wwhhoooosshh*, struck the hull of the tank, and instead of penetrating the armor, it rocketed skyward. The three Green Berets looked at each other in disbelief, and then scampered from the mortar pit to avoid the main gun fire of the tank.

Early went to the command bunker; Longgrear sent Thompson to check on Sergeant First Class Harvey Brande, whom he thought was wounded, and Longgrear moved to the flank of the tank for a better shot.

Lieutenant Colonel Daniel Schungel at the command bunker took charge of the soldiers. He shoved an armful of LAWs at each of the hastily organized tank-killer teams: First Lieutenant Wilkins, the "A" team executive officer; First Lieutenant Quy, the South Vietnamese Special Forces operations officer; Fragos; and Specialist Four McMurray.

Schungel took Longgrear with him and all of the tank-killer teams sprinted back to the perimeter to fight the tanks.

Willoughby ordered his radio operator, Specialist Four Frank Dooms, to call Da Nang and Khe Sanh to report tanks. Khe Sanh command refused to believe the sighting. Dooms spun the dials on the radio set to the artillery fire direction center frequency at Khe Sanh.

"Jacksonville, Jacksonville, this is Spunky Hansen! We are taking a heavy ground attack and have armor in the wire! Stand by for fire mission, over."

The Marines in the FDC bunker at Khe Sanh sat in stunned silence. Staff Sergeant Tom Gagnon told his radio operator to confirm the message.

"Spunky, this is Jacksonville. Are you sure about that armor?"

"Roger, roger, that is affirm. We have tanks in the perimeter!"

"Can you see them from your location?" the Marines questioned, unable to comprehend the gravity of the situation. Gagnon thought the Green Berets may have panicked.

Longgrear and Schungel met Early at the top of the steps leading to the camp's command bunker. Four sappers sprinted by. Longgrear fired at them with an automatic burst from his CAR-15 rifle killing or wounding them.

"How many LAWs do you have?" Schungel asked.

"We've got a few, but they won't fire," Longgrear shouted above the cacophony of the fight that engulfed the camp.

Inside the bunker, Willoughby tried to monitor excited cries on the radio from the OP to the west and Company 101 to the east as six more tanks descended on the camp from Highway 9.

"Get me an airstrike!" Willoughby shouted on the radio to the forward air controller who was airborne above Lang Vei.

Dooms screamed in frustration into his radio handset at the Marine artillery. "Affirmative, affirmative. I can hear the engines backfiring. They're firing into the bunkers!"

Pause. "Negative. That must be the sound of your generators backfiring."

First Lieutenant Thomas Todd, an engineer officer who arrived on 5 February to repair the Old Lang Vei air strip, was in supply bunker #1 when the attack started. A tank drove by his position enroute to the command bunker when an enemy artillery round struck his roof. He abandoned it for the emergency medical bunker. As he entered the new position, an enemy tank blasted its main gun into the entrance of the emergency medical bunker at point blank range, while another tank fired into the exit. Todd was unhurt and decided to stay in the supply bunker until first light.

The artillery showered in from Khe Sanh at last, some 17 minutes after it was requested. Marines at Khe Sanh had problems, too, although Willoughby didn't know it. The Leathernecks were receiving 152mm rounds from Co Roc in an attempt to silence their support of Lang Vei.

The Leathernecks' first salvo into the camp was completely off target, but adjustments were made over the radio and the next group of rounds roared into the enemy. The tanks had their lights turned on and they were visually sweeping the area, but artillery and small arms fire quickly extinguished the lights. The tanks fired their main guns and machine guns at the bunkers.

Sergeant First Class Bill Craig, the senior enlisted man on the "A" team, and Specialist Five Phillips were on the western portion of the perimeter. They fired illumination and high explosive rounds from the 81mm mortar at tanks moving east on Highway 9. They knew that infantry troops would not be far behind the armored vehicles.

Incoming mortar rounds impacted near their position, sending the two Green Berets to the ground. Staff Sergeant Brooks ran from his machine gun position to assist; he found the two conscious, but Craig's ears and Phillips' eyes were bleeding. Brooks remanned his gun, and Craig and Phillips began firing the 81 again.

* * *

It was now almost 0100 hours. The FAC reported to Willoughby that a Spooky flareship (C-47 fixed wing aircraft) was on station. Willoughby told him to illuminate the southern perimeter. He then grabbed the radio handset from Dooms and told Jacksonville, "We have tanks coming up the road. Request fire number five. Keep it working up and down the road."

MIKE soldiers pulled back from the eastern perimeter near the 81 pit. Sergeant First Class James Holt, on the southern perimeter, fired one of the camp's two 106mm recoilless rifles and knocked out the lead tank on Lang Troai Road. He reloaded and killed the second. Tank crews spilled from their fiery armored vehicles and CIDG troops helped Holt reload the 106 with flechette rounds, which Holt blasted at the dismounted enemy. The thousands of tiny darts hummed insanely as they sped toward their human targets. Three tanks continued their attack from the south.

Marine artillery crumped along Highway 9, stalling the northerly attack on the camp. Spooky parachuted its cargo of basketball-shaped flares over the camp, illuminating the compound in a flat, white light. Spooky radioed his concern to Willoughby that the tanks could do him harm and his Gatling guns could do little to the armored vehicles. Willoughby requested that Spooky fire on the tanks, but the pilot chose not to fly close enough to attack the tracked vehicles.

U.S. Air Force Captain Gerald L. Harrington, one of two airborne FACs over Lang Vei, peered down at the besieged camp. "It looks like the Fourth of July down there," he said to himself, "with everyone firing Roman Candles." The broken, overcast sky at 1200 feet refused leisurely scrutiny of the ground situation, where the aircraft were threatened by NVA ground fire and Marine artillery shells screamed in from Khe Sanh.

Harrington radioed Willoughby and told him his B-57 bombers carried general purpose explosives, less effective than napalm or antipersonnel rounds, but still helpful. "Where do you want them?" he asked.

"All over the south side of the hill and along the road," Willoughby replied.

"Where the flares are?"

"Yes!"

One fighter bomber accidentally dropped a bomb on Old Lang Vei. Sergeant First Class Eugene Ashley, Sergeant Allen and Specialist Four Johnson were in the old camp with the Laotian battalion, and miraculously, there were no casualties.

Willoughby received a call from Craig that the fuel dump just blew. The burning petroleum dump permitted pilots to key in on the camp, but the flares were not good enough to mark targets for the poised jet fighters. Willoughby's instructions to Harrington were imprecise and Harrington used his Starlight scope to look for tank muzzle blasts. He marked the tank locations for the fighters with white phosphorus rockets, which stuck in the ground and burned bright enough for the fighter pilots to see.

The Marines at Khe Sanh continued to receive enemy rocket and artillery fire from Co Roc Mountain. The Field Artillery Digital Automatic Computer pulsed target information to the Marines manning the guns, and the artillery batteries alternated firing to deceive the enemy guns on Co Roc. The Marine artillery batteries flashed like the fists of a boxer; a left jab, a right hook, a left and then another right.

Lieutenant Quy, the Vietnamese Special Forces operations officer at the camp, was captured by some North Vietnamese Army soldiers. He tried to make them believe he was one of them, but they did not believe him. Just as he was being led away, a fighter bomber made a low pass in the vicinity and his captors took cover. Quy ran away, hid, and later made his way to Old Lang Vei where he joined other of the camp's survivors.

Green Berets, MIKEs and CIDG inside the camp were feverish with the fight. They pumped out rounds from the 4.2-inch mortars; CIDG defenders fought hand-to-hand with NVA troops streaming through gaps in the wire; Holt squared off with a PT-76 until his ammo ran out, then abandoned his trench as enemy troops swarmed over the position. He was never seen again.

The OP reported to the command bunker that it was surrounded by NVA, and four tanks and two platoons of enemy infantry were moving west on Highway 9 to the camp. Moments later, Companies 102 and 103 repelled an infantry assault. The NVA foot soldiers backed off and let the tanks through.

By 0130 hours, the outer perimeter and eastern side of the camp caved in. The four tanks from the west crushed the defenses of Companies 102 and 103. CIDG reported the enemy attacking with fresh bandages applied, apparently determined to take Lang Vei at any cost. The tanks fired main gun blasts at point blank range into CIDG defenders. It was a slaughter. Survivors retreated northward toward Highway 9 and ran into the impenetrable NVA ring around the camp.

Harrington's white phosphorus rocket markers burned near three tanks he saw firing into the command bunker. He summoned a twin jet, medium B-57 bomber from above the clouds.

The plane banked in and dropped four bombs on the mark, which triggered some 15 secondary explosions. Harrington counted three destroyed tanks.

The radio in the command bunker sputtered and crackled. Hanna reported from the OP that Sergeant First Class Lindewald was seriously wounded. "Charlie's been hit in the gut! He's pretty bad...we're being overrun!" The radio static blared momentarily and then was silent. Communications with the OP was lost at 0230 hours.

Craig, Staff Sergeant Tiroch and some 50 CIDG were pushed toward the northeastern part of the camp. They evaded through the wire as machine gun bullets tore the air around them, and they split up outside the wire. The two Americans moved 100 meters north of the defensive wire to a clump of bamboo. A cluster bomb unit wounded them and they crawled another 200 meters to a dry creek bed where they stayed until first light.

A blast from a PT-76's main gun struck the command bunker door and showered debris inward. Inside the bunker, Specialist Four

Moreland lay blinded, with his hands mangled. Wilkins was wounded when 55-gallon drums filled with dirt toppled on him from the force of the blast.

Early and Longgrear were sent sprawling inside the bunker and Schungel, above ground, was knocked off his feet. Schungel quickly recovered, grabbed two grenades, and charged the approaching tank amid a shower of enemy machine gun fire. Longgrear told Willoughby inside the bunker that Schungel was killed in the blast.

The command bunker's exits had caved in. Trapped in the bunker with Willoughby were Longgrear, Brooks, Phillips, Early, Fragos, Dooms, and the seriously wounded Moreland. The South Vietnamese camp commander and sergeant major, the commander of Company 104, 1 interpreter and some 30 CIDG were also entombed with the Americans.

Schungel and Wilkins, still above ground, fled to the teamhouse at approximately 0300 hours. Five NVA armed with AK-47s and satchel charges approached the teamhouse, and died in a hail of M-16 fire from Schungel. A charge went off, wounding Schungel in the right leg, and he and Wilkins crept undetected to the dispensary, where they hid under the wooden floor boards until morning.

By 0300 hours, the tank-killer teams on the ground continued their desperate struggle. Willoughby decided it was time to play his aces. He radioed Khe Sanh command and asked the Marines to activate their rehearsed relief plan of Lang Vei.

Marine radio operators at Khe Sanh sat in a sober silence as their radio speakers coughed Willoughby's request. "Americans are dying up here. For Christ's sake, help us!"

The Marines refused.

The young Leatherneck company commanders and platoon leaders wanted to go. It was the high ranking Marine commanders in Da Nang who would not comply with the request.

Intelligence gathered by the fighters in the skies over Lang Vei, and transmitted to Khe Sanh, indicated that several tanks had withdrawn from the Special Forces camp to likely helicopter landing zones, which would preclude an assault by air. Sending relief troops over land would get them butchered, the Marines decided. General Westmoreland, in Saigon, was consulted.

The Marines said no again.

Colonel Jonathan Ladd, commander of Special Forces in Vietnam, tried to intervene. Westmoreland allowed his commanders closest to the action decide. The Marines stayed put. By first light, Westmoreland was on a plane to Da Nang to confer with U.S. Marine Corps Lieutenant General Cushman on the state of the Tet Offensive in I Corps.

Special Forces headquarters in Da Nang received calls from "A" teams in other areas who volunteered to relieve Lang Vei. The MIKE Force at Da Nang requested helicopters to fly them in. The entire complement of personnel from Project Delta, a classified reconnaissance unit, offered to go in and rescue their friends.

None were allowed to go.

Major Adam Husar, the MIKE Force battalion commander for I Corps, rallied nearly 150 of his Montagnard troops at Da Nang upon hearing of enemy tanks at Lang Vei. The relief force scurried aboard C-130s at dawn and flew to Quang Tri, where they were grounded to await further orders, and transportation, to make a heliborne assault on the camp, "right down the chimney."

The relief force sat on the runway at Quang Tri while Westmoreland flew to Da Nang from Saigon to confer with his subordinate commanders.

* * *

The confident NVA soldiers gathered outside the sealed command bunker. The enemy took their time. A tank rolled on top of the bunker and ground down on the roof to collapse it. The roof held.

But the communications did not. Willoughby lost his radio link to Khe Sanh as the tank broke off his antennas. The splintered antennas and weakened radio batteries permitted only short range communication now.

Sergeant First Class Gene Ashley, a bespectacled Green Beret medic, flown in to tend to the Laotians at Old Lang Vei, radioed Willoughby from the former camp. He told the captain he had rallied some Laotians and would come to their aid.

Throughout the night, the Lao battalion commander refused to get involved in the fight. NVA commanders shouted into the night from

Lang Vei to the old camp that the Laotians should not help. The Lao battalion commander steadfastly refused to help, but eventually relented under Ashley's insistence; he let two platoons of his troops go with the Americans.

Ashley called in an airstrike to cover his advance and charged the eastern perimeter of Lang Vei. As the ragtag force neared the Company 104 area, NVA machinegunners thundered their rage at Ashley's army. The Laotians broke and ran. Enraged, Ashley ran them down and, amid NVA mortar fire, rallied them again.

Willoughby tried desperately with Dooms to re-establish radio contact with Khe Sanh. Fragos tended to the shattered and delirious Moreland. Moreland thought his friends in the bunker were the enemy and threatened to kill them until Longgrear tackled him and Fragos administered morphine. The powerful pain killer is deadly when given to an individual with a head wound, but they had no choice. Moreland slumped to the ground and went unconscious. The soldiers in the command bunker heard the bark of NVA weapons as they answered Ashley's attempt to throw the enemy from Lang Vei.

It was daylight now and with night gone, the NVA renewed its efforts at unearthing the barricaded defenders of Lang Vei. They clawed at the bunker, taped satchel charges to the walls and then threw tear gas and thermite grenades down the bunker airshafts to ignite debris inside.

Shreds of map paper and documents inside the bunker burned and smoldered for 30 minutes, and spewed a choking cloud of smoke throughout the small room.

The soldiers inside huddled on the floor and buried their noses in small crevices near the bottom of the walls, or into the few gas protective masks available, and clawed for fresh air. Those without masks covered their noses and mouths with battle dressings to filter the stench as NVA soldiers dropped tear gas grenades down the air shafts. The defenders choked and vomited.

Willoughby felt the end was near. He ordered classified documents and codes to be destroyed. An Oriental voice called down the stairs in Vietnamese for the defenders to surrender. "We are going to destroy the bunker. Give up and we will not harm you," the interpreter translated to Willoughby.

Stunned, scared faces turned toward the door. A couple of tired smiles appeared. Somebody whispered, "Fuck you."

The VNSF commander hastily conferred with his subordinates and then forced the door open. He led his soldiers up the stairs to the waiting enemy.

One of the eight Americans left in the bunker bolted the door shut. Another demand for surrender echoed down the cordite burned staircase, followed by a shower of grenades. The Americans didn't budge. A volley of gunfire shattered the white morning mists outside and signaled the execution of the surrendering Vietnamese. The NVA tried once more to kill the Americans in the bunker.

The Green Berets became quiet in an attempt to play possum. Perhaps if the enemy thought they were dead they would leave. Just in case, though, the Americans readied themselves. By 0700 hours, they pooled their ammunition, smeared off the gunk caked on the bullets, snapped links together to lengthen belts of machine gun ammunition, and trained the barrels of their weapons on the door awaiting the *Final Charge.*

A symphony of explosive charges on the south wall disintegrated an eight-foot square section of the bunker and knocked the eight Americans unconscious. Moreland's shattered body suffered more brutal wounds. An ugly gash opened on the side of Longgrear's head despite the steel helmet that he wore, and his blood spilled on the blackened, littered floor. The Americans waited again for the *Final Charge.*

It never came. The NVA commander's attention again turned toward the camp's eastern perimeter as another airstrike preceded Ashley's second attempt to liberate his compatriots.

Craig and Tiroch rallied some CIDG who fled the camp with them during the night, and joined Ashley's assault. Enemy mortar rounds coughed from the camp and splintered Ashley's assembly area. The reluctant soldiers pressed on toward the camp when an NVA company counterattacked the ragtag group. They fell back once more as Ashley radioed Willoughby, "It's no good. I'm getting a lot of fire and we're taking a lot of casualties. I'm gonna try again."

Ashley's force was now reduced by half. An enemy mortar misfired and the soldiers used this pause to gain some ground against the well-entrenched NVA. They were repelled for a third time and then a fourth. The sick and disheartened band of soldiers retreated toward the road to rest.

Johnson had scrounged a 57-millimeter recoilless rifle and silenced the machine gun near the bunker. This brief victory lifted friendly enthusiasm for the battle and the group surged forward into the NVA held trenches. Ashley was mortally wounded in the chest from small arms fire. The enemy, seeing the American down, rallied and stopped Ashley's army 50 meters short of the command bunker.

Hope flickered for an instant in the entombed soldiers' eyes as the rifle fire drew closer. The hope winked out as they realized the fifth attempt to liberate them had failed.

Schungel and Wilkins hobbled out from under the vacated dispensary at 0930 hours. They saw two burned-out tank hulls a few meters to the west that had apparently been hit by the fighter bombers and were reduced to rubble. The two soldiers crossed Highway 9, where a mortar round impacted and wounded Schungel again. A CIDG soldier came to help and the three moved to Old Lang Vei.

Ashley was carried to Highway 9 where Johnson and Allen gave him first aid. A jeep sent for Schungel appeared from the brush and the medics jumped aboard. They put Ashley on the jeep and started back to Old Lang Vei. Barely inside the wire of the camp, a mortar round shattered the jeep, wounding Allen and killing Ashley.

Westmoreland, now in Da Nang, was disturbed by the developments in I Corps. He called together his Marine and Army commanders, listened to their reports, and gave orders to reopen roads, establish new logistics lines, and to move troops to meet an enemy thrust in Da Nang.

He ordered the Marines to reinforce at Hue, and he ordered them to provide helicopters to extract the survivors at Lang Vei.

Inside the rubble strewn command bunker, the defenders felt a last pang of dread as they learned of Ashley's death. The enemy no longer feared a ground attack from the east, but jet fighters kept their heads down.

The Green Berets inside the bunker were now delirious with thirst and exhaustion, and their parched hopes screamed for a decision. All were wounded two or three times. Each carried less than six magazines for his M-16. One carried only a pistol, his CAR-15 having been twisted and shattered into an odd, useless sculpture.

Willoughby learned from his fragile radio via Old Lang Vei that forces in Da Nang would try a rescue attempt "if they could hold out one more night."

Longgrear said, "No way," and limped toward the door in a half-hearted attempt to leave. Willoughby called him back and the seven conscious Green Berets in the bunker conferred. It was late afternoon now and they had gone without food, water or rest for 18 hours. They had endured countless explosions ripping through the concrete bunker. They were weak from loss of blood and dehydrated from no food or water. They needed medical attention for their wounds.

They needed out.

Each man took a few moments to prepare for their escape. They hurriedly cleaned their few bullets to prevent their weapons from jamming. They tightened field bandages around their wounds and straightened the pins of their grenades for easier pulling. They scratched catholes in the dirt floor and buried ID cards and dogtags so the NVA could not identify their bodies and claim them as POWs.

They also decided to leave Moreland behind. They were all sick and wounded, and Moreland was so badly injured he probably wouldn't make it. It was a difficult decision to make, but they felt they had no choice.

Willoughby radioed Air Force pilots overhead, via Old Lang Vei, with their escape plans. Make three "hot" runs at the camp, he said, and then "dry" runs to keep NVA heads down. At that point, we'll run.

The pilots, who had pounded the ground above the command bunker continuously throughout the battle, complied. Shock waves vaulted through the bunker, and sent debris and dirt through the putrid air. After the third "hot" run by the jets, the Americans unbolted the door to the command bunker, stumbled over stacked bodies in the staircase, and with Longgrear at point, filed upstairs.

The volley of weapons fire they expected from the enemy did not come. The Americans hobbled into the late afternoon sun and headed across open ground to the east.

An enemy machine gun thundered at the column and Longgrear, who was on point, answered with a burst from his CAR-15; he silenced the threat. They continued a little farther when Longgrear glimpsed two enemy soldiers pilfering the pockets of dead MIKE Force soldiers. Longgrear left the column and charged the two.

As he engaged them, his painful ankle went out from under him and his rifle jammed. The six walking wounded thought he had been shot and continued their march.

Longgrear lay sprawled on the ground and for an instant, he thought he saw his own death. Jets overhead seemed to stop in midair and he heard nothing. A soul-comforting calm settled over him and then, just as quickly as it had come, the sound returned to his ears and the jets resumed their flight.

Longgrear used his rifle as a brace and struggled to his feet. The enemy did not fire. He rejoined the battered column and led it toward the perimeter as a jeep thundered up to them from a path. It was Quy, speeding from Old Lang Vei behind the jeep's wheel, "the bravest thing I've ever seen a man do in combat," Longgrear said later.

The grateful Americans piled aboard and Quy sped off for the old camp. Longgrear saw the faces of NVA set up in the brush along the road in an ambush site. The enemy watched, mesmerized. They did not fire!

They were almost out.

Three Marine CH-46 helicopters circled over Lang Vei, unwilling to descend in the threat of NVA ground fire. A command and control helicopter, a smaller UH-1B model, with Major Quamo aboard, who was the commander of FOB-3, lost patience with the larger troop-carrying pilots' stubbornness, swooped out of the sky, touched ground amid swarms of CIDG, MIKE soldiers, and Laotian troops clamoring aboard.

Sometime shortly after the breakout, 1LT Todd stumbled down the stairs into the command bunker. He saw the awful mess and turned to leave. It was then he saw Moreland, checked him out, and determined that the young medic was dead. He quickly moved back up the stairs and sprinted to the eastern perimeter of the camp. As he crossed the tangled wire marking the edge of the camp, enemy small fire raked at him from behind. He was unhit, and continued his cross country run to the safety of the old camp.

*   *   *

Longgrear, in pain and delirious from thirst and exhaustion, pointed his jammed CAR-15 at a group of panicking Laotian soldiers climbing aboard the helicopter at Old Lang Vei. They took a few steps backward, not realizing his weapon would not fire. The most stubborn allies, many of whom had not assisted the Americans in the bunker, had laced their wrists through the webbed seating in an attempt to guarantee their passage aboard the helicopter. Longgrear lashed out with his rifle at their arms, smashing their wrists with his rifle butt and dislodging them from the aircraft. He then helped pile the wounded American defenders aboard.

Once aloft, the CH-46s landed to scoop up the allies and fly some of them to safety. The rest had to walk the eight kilometers to the Khe Sanh combat base.

The command and control helicopter set down moments later at the Marine base at Khe Sanh. The Americans spilled from the aircraft, several of whom were too overcome with exhaustion and the delicious euphoria of having survived a battle in which they had resigned themselves to certain death.

Longgrear took a couple of painful hobbles and fell as his weight became too much for his shattered ankle. An unknown Marine pulled him up and slung Longgrear's arm around his shoulder, easing him towards Charlie Med, the medical bunker at Khe Sanh. An Associated Press photographer clicked his shutter at the pair, his first glimpse at what journalists would chronicle as the "vacant, horror-filled stares of the survivors of Lang Vei." The photo would grace morning U.S. newspaper front pages and the next issue of *Newsweek* magazine.

The battle for Lang Vei was over.

138

An unidentified US Marine assists wounded US Army First Lieutenant Paul R. Longgrear at the Khe Sanh Combat Base after Longgrear was evacuated from Lang Vei on 7 February 1968.

Photo courtesy of World Wide Photos

The Army Special Forces camp at Lang Vei the morning after being over-run, showing one demolished North Vietnamese Army tank outside the ruined command bunker where several Special Forces soldiers held out.

Author's collection

Lang Vei as it appeared on the morning after the attack, showing the destroyed bunker lines.

Photo courtesy of Shelby L. Stanton

A US Army 1st Cavalry Division soldier advances on the burned-out hull of a PT-76 tank at Lang Vei during Operation Pegasus in April, 1968, two months after the NVA used tanks for the first time in the Vietnam war.

Photo courtesy of Wide World Photos

12

After Action Report

Elements of the North Vietnamese Army's 304th Division attacked and overran the Lang Vei Special Forces camp on 7 February 1968. The force used 11 Soviet-made PT-76 amphibious tanks and approximately 400 dismounted infantry troops. Supporting fires consisted of an estimated four 152-millimeter artillery pieces and four 82-millimeter mortars.

Enemy losses were estimated to have been seven tanks (confirmed) and two tanks (probable), and 250 infantry soldiers killed in action.

The Lang Vei anti-tank weapons consisted of two 106-millimeter recoilless rifles and approximately eighty-five LAWs. Friendly statistics were:

Before battle		WIA	KIA/MIA
U.S. Special Forces -	24	13	10
VNSF -	14	3	5
CIDG -	282	29	165
MIKE Force -	196	32	34
Interpreters -	6	0	5
Totals:	**522**	**77**	**219**

The after action report noted that despite inadequate tank defenses and lack of psychological conditioning for an armored attack, the CIDG and MIKE Force put up a spirited defense and did not break and run. Well over half of the CIDG force died in defense of their positions, actually trying to fight tanks with machine guns, carbines and rifles.

The report recommended all CIDG camps include anti-tank training for all personnel, to include the construction of tank obstacles. One further recommendation was that CIDG camps with areas of operation contiguous to other countries, must provide thorough reconnaissance across those borders to ensure timely and accurate reports of enemy locations and early warning of impending attacks.

The camp defenses at Lang Vei stopped the attack; it could not move beyond the camp to Khe Sanh. Lang Vei's position could have been restored had the Lao battalion been more aggressive, or if the MIKE Force on the runway at Quang Tri had been given adequate transportation to perform a heliborne assault.

Or if the Marines at Khe Sanh had been allowed to initiate their rehearsed relief of the camp.

Officially, the Marines ignored any connection between Lang Vei and Khe Sanh. The Summary of 1968 actions published in Saigon by the United States Military Assistance Command's Office of Information describes the battle this way:

> "...the defenders were compelled to withdraw from the camp under pressure. The North Vietnamese forces used several tanks in the attack...This was the first enemy employment of armor in the war and was a failure."

The logbook of the First Battalion/26th Marines for February 1968 does not mention the fall of Lang Vei.

A USMC film featuring Colonel David Lownds, 26th Marine Regiment commander, explaining the Siege of Khe Sanh on a terrain model table, made no mention of the potential armor threat on the combat base or of the artillery support for the Special Forces at Lang Vei.

Unofficially, the Marines at Khe Sanh felt the psychological bite of the attacking tanks. They re-read firing instructions labeled on the side of the LAW tubes and stockpiled armor-piercing bullets near their .50-caliber machine guns.

Young Marines on the edges of the besieged combat base sat out long, terrified night watches. One war-awed correspondent captured their emotions this way:

> "After Lang Vei, how could you look out of your perimeter at night without hearing the treads coming? How could you patrol in the dark without remembering every story you ever heard about ghostly enemy helicopters flying the fringes of the Z? About the trail cut in the floor of the A Shau Valley, big enough to hold trucks? About the complete fanaticism of attackers who were doped to the eyeballs (sure they smoke dope, it gets them crazy), who ran pushing civilian shields forward, who chained themselves to their machine guns rather than fail, who had No Regard for Human Life?"

The Siege of the Khe Sanh combat base continued for 77 days. It ended in a relief effort, codenamed Operation Pegasus, by the U.S. Army First Cavalry Division on April Fool's Day 1968. The enemy had never attacked the base in the expected magnitude and many felt it had been a non-siege. Marine commanders demanded that Pegasus should not implicate "a rescue or breaking of the siege by outside forces."

Theories on the enemy's intentions for Khe Sanh continue to be clouded in disagreement. Many military experts believe Khe Sanh was a feint to tie down the Marines while enemy units sidestepped the base to attack cities on the coast. Sir Robert Thompson, a British military analyst and counterinsurgency expert, believed, "One of the reasons why General Giap did not attack Khe Sanh (is) he did not want to awaken in the American people an overriding emotion of patriotism in support of the war."

General William C. Westmoreland said, "There were two enemy divisions around Khe Sanh and part of a third waiting in the wings...facing *one* reinforced American regiment of about 6,000 men.

"How could anyone legitimately question who was tying down whom?"

General Vo Nguyen Giap described Khe Sanh this way: "Dien Bien Phu, Dien Bien Phu, look. It's not always true that history repeats itself. Khe Sanh didn't try to be, nor could it have been, a Dien Bien

Phu. Khe Sanh wasn't that important to us.

"Besides, don't you think we won at Khe Sanh?

"I say, yes."

A radio broadcast from Hanoi monitored in Tokyo on February 9, and reported by the Associated Press, reads:

"North Vietnam says Khe Sanh will be another Dien Bien Phu."

The fight for Hue continued from 31 January until 25 February before Friendly Forces' colors flew over the Citadel, replacing the red, blue, and gold-star banner of the NVA. It was the first real urban fighting in the war and several city blocks of the Imperial City were reduced to rubble. The threat at Quang Tri was also repelled. The enemy's attempt to secure northern South Vietnam failed militarily.

The twenty-six-day battle for Hue was perhaps the bloodiest of the Tet Offensive. Its proximity allowed correspondents to literally drive to the action in the morning and return to their cold beer and hot steaks in the evening. The situation lent itself to wide news coverage and made a substantial impact on public opinion in the United States.

The facts of the battle for Hue were literally unearthed in the months following the action, but received far less attention. The bodies of 2,800 civilians, victims of North Vietnamese aggression, were found in graves dug in school yards, parks and jungle creek beds. They had been rounded up by the NVA, forcibly removed from their homes, and were shot to death, bludgeoned, or buried alive in an attempt at political genocide.

The publicity of the Tet Offensive in the United States, which was examined in chapter four, destroyed the credibility of American officials who sought to inform their countrymen that we were winning militarily during the Tet Offensive, that the communist aggression had been repelled; these officials were not believed.

The Tet Offensive succeeded in turning around American support of the war in Vietnam. One in five Americans at home who supported the war before Tet had shifted against the war by the first week in April 1968. It cost Westmoreland his bid for an additional quarter-of-a-million U.S. troops to join his more than half-million soldier force in Vietnam.

The Marines' refusal to relieve the district headquarters or Lang Vei, previously ordered and rehearsed contingencies, was one key element in the later decision to replace them with U.S. Army soldiers at Khe Sanh.

The Marines lost political favor by that nonaction. From the beginning, Marine commanders felt they should not have been at Khe Sanh. Then, when things went out of control, they felt victimized by the consequences of their decisions. It is a controversy that will never be settled.

Lang Vei also contains its share of controversies.

One of the personnel assigned to the 106-millimeter recoilless rifle departed the camp on 6 February. A replacement was not designated. Had someone been assigned that position, it is possible the western perimeter of the camp might have repelled, or at least stalled, the tank assault on Companies 102 and 103.

The Lang Vei Special Forces soldier captured by the NVA on 30 January, John Young, later discovered he was suspected of providing information on the camp to the enemy. Survivors of the battle of Lang Vei have differing opinions.

Some acknowledge that he could not have known much about the camp, since he arrived at Old Lang Vei three days before his capture. Young maintains this position, also.

During his captivity, though, Young incurred disfavor with his fellow prisoners by his outspoken criticism of U.S. involvement in Southeast Asia. He was one of five prisoners, dubbed the "Peace Committee," who allegedly cooperated with the enemy in a variety of propaganda activities and received favorable treatment by the enemy.

All five were charged with misconduct at the war's end. Secretary of the Army, Howard H. Callaway, dismissed those charges against the five on 3 July 1973.

One of the speculations about how the fate of Lang Vei could have been altered will never be answered. Major Adam Husar and his company of MIKE Force were armed and ready to perform a heliborne assault into the camp. They flew from Da Nang at first light and waited on the runway at Quang Tri.

They flew to Quang Tri in an airplane and could not get the helicopters necessary to assault the camp. The official report states: "The Mobile Strike Force company which had moved to Quang Tri to reinforce the camp, could not be displaced further due to a lack of helicopters."

If ever a man had been robbed of his moment in history, it is Husar. After all, Longgrear was one of his company commanders. The MIKE soldiers on the OP and in the camp were his soldiers; he was their battalion commander and led their fellow soldiers in the relief effort.

At Quang Tri, with his troops deposited on the runway, he pleaded for transportation, he screamed for helicopters to take him and his troops in. Paradoxically, the one man who most wanted to reinforce Lang Vei, who commanded nearly half of the besieged indigenous soldiers in the camp, did not get closer than 90 miles from the action.

The relief force quietly returned to Da Nang that evening.

It is also puzzling to discern why amphibious tanks were used at that time and place. Robert Pisor, an author and authority on the Siege of Khe Sanh, sums it up this way:

> "I always thought it was a P.R. attack, more for show and shock than for effectiveness. The NVA loved "surprise" almost to the extent of bizarre, and it was, after all, effective. Thin-skinned pawns sacrificed to take a knight, and headlines, too.
>
> "The paucity of main battle tanks, the difficulty of transportation, (especially in the bomb rain of Khe Sanh)...but most of all, the imperative need to have mobile muscle at home, where the Yanks might try to invade, were all factors in no MBTs at Lang Vei."

The enemy's views may never be known. This author's letters to the defense ministry and General Vo Nguyen Giap, mailed directly to them and also through the Vietnamese ambassador to the United Nations in New York, and through the Australian ambassador to the Socialist Republic of Vietnam in Hanoi, went unanswered and were never returned.

CONCLUSIONS

The attack on the Special Forces camp at Lang Vei was the first use of enemy armor in the Vietnam war. Although the tanks were thin skinned vehicles primarily developed for reconnaissance and not decisive engagements, it was clear the North Vietnamese did not maximize their use. Had the tanks concentrated on one side of the perimeter with fire and maneuver instead of the fragmented flanking movement the NVA attempted in the awkward, hilly terrain, the camp might have been overrun with less loss of enemy life.

It would be safe to assume the NVA knew the power of the artillery at Khe Sanh and that the guns would fire support for the Green Berets. Perhaps the tanks were split up for the assault because of the artillery threat.

The use of tanks at Lang Vei was for shock, which it achieved. Even though the Lang Vei camp was overrun, the enemy sustained heavier losses than it anticipated. Had the losses not been so great, it seems clear that the NVA would have employed the tanks on an assault at the Marine Corps Combat Base at Khe Sanh to either seriously try to overrun the base, as American officials expected, or to draw more Free World troops and resources away from the fighting in the coastal cities.

The American concept of the operations at the Khe Sanh Combat Base and the Special Forces Camp remains unclear. The intent in establishing a stronghold at Khe Sanh was to block a large scale infiltration of NVA troops from Laos. The defense of the combat base centered on the American footholds on the hills surrounding the base. General Westmoreland thought he could lure the NVA into a conventional battle at Khe Sanh, one in which the Americans would win with superior firepower.

Why was Lang Vei not abandoned earlier? If it was intended to be another observation point for the Khe Sanh Combat Base, it most likely would have been integrated better into the communications network at the base. Perhaps it was used to help lure the NVA into the fight.

Perhaps there was no clear concept for Lang Vei to exist at all.

As the Tet Offensive took shape, it seems as though the role of the tiny camp at Lang Vei played an integral part of the shift in NVA tactics in northern South Vietnam. Originally, the NVA used the Tet Offensive as a surprise attack, a seemingly overwhelming assault, on the entire country of South Vietnam.

Then, the culturally important city of Hue came under attack, and the Khe Sanh Combat Base came under siege. As the Americans fought viciously in Hue, the NVA stepped up its siege of Khe Sanh in an attempt to draw more men and resources away from Hue. Part of that plan included the tank attack on Lang Vei, an attack so devastating in its shock, the Americans would have to order more soldiers out to the west.

But the NVA lost more than it bargained for at Lang Vei, and shortly after the attack on the camp, NVA units previously reported as fighting at Khe Sanh, were identified fighting in Hue. NVA General Vo Nguyen Giap later claimed he never intended to assault Khe Sanh at all, the siege of the combat base was a ruse, a feint, designed to keep the Americans off-guard as to his actual objective: Hue.

Despite the lack of a clear concept for the American operations at the Lang Vei Special Forces camp, as it related to the Marines, the tank attack illuminated serious flaws in Marine-Army relationships. Westmoreland used U.S. Army soldiers to relieve the Marine combat base, and then established the U.S. Army XXIV Corps at Hue to control the northern part of South Vietnam.

* * *

The most dramatic consequences of the battle of Lang Vei involved its participants:

U.S. Army Major George Quamo, the FOB-3 commander at the Khe Sanh Combat Base, who orchestrated the helicopter rescue of the survivors, died in an aircraft crash a few months later. His body was recovered in 1974.

Lieutenant Quy, the VNSF operations officer at Lang Vei who drove the jeep through visible ambush sites to retrieve the seven Americans as they escaped from the command bunker, was also killed in action a few months later.

First Lieutenant Paul Longgrear, the MIKE Force commander at Lang Vei, had a spiritual conversion to Jesus during the tank battle (which he tells in a later chapter in this book); this experience made him leave active duty in several years to pursue a spiritually rewarding career as a minister, and he is also a Lieutenant Colonel, US Army

Reserve.

Staff Sergeant Dennis L. Thompson, whom Longgrear sent to check on **Sergeant First Class Harvey G. Brande** early in the battle, was later captured along with Brande by the NVA. On 18 February, 1968, the two escaped their captors, but Brande was too badly wounded in both legs, his right hand, his chest and his head.

Thompson carried Brande and nursed his wounds as best he could, until finally Brande ordered Thompson to abandon him and escape toward friendly forces. Thompson refused and the two were recaptured soon thereafter. Upon repatriation at the end of the war, the two POWs received Silver Stars and other decorations for their valor at Lang Vei.

* * *

One unsubstantiated, but intriguing, report exists. A 12-man detachment was reported to have been sent from FOB-3 to Lang Vei consisting of members of a SOG team. The team was sent after the Marine refusal to reinforce the Lang Vei camp, and the team was ambushed near Khe Sanh Village. Only three members of the team survived, and they were held prisoner in Laos for eight months until a heliborne assault on their POW camp rescued them.

* * *

Three days after Lang Vei, USMC Staff Sergeant Thomas "Jim" Gagnon found a moment to write that letter home from the Khe Sanh Combat Base. Despite statistical inaccuracies, which he believed to be true at the time, it was a poignant message:

> "We lost one camp three days ago...there were 500 men there, we got four out. The North Vietnamese used tanks there and we could not stop them all. We got three of them anyhow.
> "The camp was a Special Forces camp of Lang Vei. We fired over 3,000 rounds on the Vietnamese. They attacked

our camp two days ago, we left their dead all over the wire...

"I am going to send you receipts of the money I have saved on the ten percent plan so you can take care of them (his children) for me...How are the children? I think most of all I miss them more and more all the time. Take care of them for me no matter what...you have all my other papers, everything should be in order now...I will write again when I get a chance."

Your son,
Jim

Gagon's mother kept that letter. "He hardly ever wrote," she said, her wrinkled eyes recalling the despair she had long suppressed, "and when I got that letter I knew he felt certain he was going to die."

* * *

The fate of the Bru Montagnards was perhaps the saddest of all. After Lang Vei fell, some 6,000 Bru and Lao refugees, many of them soldiers, descended on the gate of the Khe Sanh Combat Base. Fearful of a modern day Trojan Horse, with no accurate measure to determine patriot from infiltrator, and certainly not enough food, medicine and housing to care for them, the U.S. Marines disarmed the refugees at the gate and turned them out.

They headed east to homestead at Mai Loc, and some of them were airlifted to Qui Nhon via Air America, until they returned to Khe Sanh in the spring of 1970. By then, American soldiers were leaving the Khe Sanh Plateau for the last time.

The more observant and cynical Montagnards who saw the Americans early on build their accommodations with temporary sandbags and tin siding, bitterly saw their vision of abandonment become reality.

* * *

One final note that followed the battle of Lang Vei involves the fears of the soldiers' families back home. The following is an excerpt from a letter written by Colonel Fred O. Jackson, Longgrear's father-in-law, to Delta Airlines on 9 February 1968. It represents the anguish all families must have felt.

"My daughter is making her home with us in Columbus, Georgia while her husband is in Vietnam. For the past two days my daughter had been most concerned because her husband, 1st Lt. Paul R. Longgrear, a Special Forces advisor, was at Lang Vie (sic) when that camp was overrun by the Viet Cong, and only a small number of American advisors escaped.

"Last night my daughter received a telephone call from Jonesboro, Arkansas and was told her husband's picture was in the local paper. No name was given, but the caption stated that the wounded soldier was one who escaped and made his way to friendly forces after Lang Vei (sic) fell.

"Needless to say, my daughter wanted to see that picture to assure herself that her husband was alive. After a search of all papers at the local newsstands, I decided to see what airlines served Jonesboro. I called Delta Airlines and talked to Miss Jan Newton. I told her the situation and stated that I was willing to purchase a ticket if a copy of the Jonesboro *Sun* paper could be checked through for me.

"Miss Newton asked that I speak to her supervisor, Mr. Buck Spearman. (He) called me back and told me he had arranged to get a copy of the newspaper...and that Delta representatives would get it to Columbus on flight #427 arriving at 7:04.

"This morning, a copy of the Jonesboro, Arkansas *Evening Sun* arrived on the 7:04 a.m. Delta flight. My daughter was delighted to see her husband's picture on the front page. Although wounded and in pain, Lieutenant Longgrear was on his feet and still holding his M-16 rifle..."

13

Roll Call:
Awards and Decorations

The following list of members of A-101, the American cadre of the MIKE Force at Lang Vei, and the Special Forces soldiers assigned to assist the Laotians at Old Lang Vei includes each individual's status following the tank battle and some of the awards they earned. Comments on some of the individuals are remembrances by the survivors of the battle who contributed to this book.

The most notable awards and decorations include the following:

The **U.S. Navy Presidential Unit Citation** was awarded to the U.S. Army Special Forces Detachment A-101 for actions during the battle of Lang Vei, Huong Hoa District, Quang Tri Province, Republic of Vietnam, 7 February 1968.

The **Medal of Honor** was posthumously awarded to **U.S. Army Special Forces Sergeant First Class Eugene Ashley** for his actions in trying to repel the North Vietnamese Army assault on Lang Vei by rallying indigenous and Laotian soldiers in a counterattack effort. Ashley was killed on his *fifth* attempt to counterattack the camp from Old Lang Vei.

The **Distinguished Service Cross** was awarded to **U.S. Army Special Forces Lieutenant Colonel Daniel F. Schungel**, who organized tank killer teams during the battle of Lang Vei. His fellow soldiers last saw him during the action charging a tank with only two hand grenades. He survived.

A-101

Captain Frank C. Willoughby, commander, Wounded In Action. Willoughby was trapped in the command bunker at Lang Vei until the breakout during the afternoon of 7 February 1968. He was later awarded **the Silver Star, the Vietnamese Cross of Gallantry, Bronze Award, and the Purple Heart**. He was an infantry officer, older than most captains, "who was very solid and brave, but cautious; very much in charge of his team."

First Lieutenant Miles Wilkins, executive officer, Wounded In Action. Wilkins hid with Schungel under the wooden floor of the camp dispensary after receiving his wounds when the camp was overrun, and later evaded to Old Lang Vei. He was awarded **the Purple Heart**. His team members remember him as, "young and enthusiastic, a team player."

Sergeant First Class William T. Craig, team sergeant, Wounded In Action. Craig and Sergeant Dan Phillips defended the western perimeter of the camp with mortar fire, although wounded, until the North Vietnamese tanks and infantry troops forced them to escape and evade through the northeastern perimeter wire to Old Lang Vei, where they assisted Sergeant Eugene Ashley in his final, and fatal attempt, to counterattack the camp. Craig had eight years in Special Forces at the time, with one year in Laos and two previous tours in Vietnam prior to the battle of Lang Vei. He was awarded **the Silver Star, the Vietnamese Cross of Gallantry, Bronze Award, and the Purple Heart** for his actions at Lang Vei. He is remembered as, "a tremendous individual who spent only four days away from the Lang Vei site from September 1967 until the tank battle." Craig is now a retired Command Sergeant Major.

Sergeant First Class James Holt, medic, **Missing In Action**. His fellow soldiers last saw him defending the southeastern perimeter of the camp, where he fired a 106-millimeter recoilless rifle at the assaulting tanks until he ran out of ammunition.

Sergeant First Class Kenneth Hanna, weapons specialist, **Missing In Action**. Hanna was with Sergeant First Class Charles Lindewald on the observation point when their position was overrun early in the battle. He was considered to be, "a brave soldier who was liked by all."

Staff Sergeant Peter Tiroch, intelligence specialist, Wounded In Action. Tiroch defended the center of the camp with LAW and .50-caliber machine gun fire until he ran out of ammunition. Once the command bunker was entombed, he evaded through the northern perimeter wire to Old Lang Vei, where he continued to assist in counterattack efforts although wounded. He was later awarded **the Vietnamese Cross of Gallantry, Bronze Award, and the Purple Heart**. He is remembered as, "young, ambitious and in excellent physical condition." He is thought to be an officer now and still on active duty.

Staff Sergeant Emmanuel E. Phillips, radio operator, Wounded In Action. Phillips was trapped in the command bunker at Lang Vei until the breakout during the afternoon of 7 February 1968. He was later awarded **the Vietnamese Cross of Gallantry, Bronze Award, and the Purple Heart** for his actions at Lang Vei. He is remembered as, "a quiet individual who got along well with everyone in the team." Phillips was reportedly killed in an accident in 1969 at Fort Bragg, North Carolina.

Staff Sergeant Arthur Brooks, weapons specialist, Wounded In Action. Brooks was trapped in the command bunker at Lang Vei until the breakout during the afternoon of 7 February 1968. He was later awarded **the Vietnamese Cross of Gallantry, Bronze Award, and the Purple Heart** for his actions at Lang Vei.

Staff Sergeant Dennis L. Thompson, radio operator, Wounded In Action and prisoner of war. Thompson, later a Sergeant First Class, was captured with Sergeant First Class Harvey G. Brande during the battle of Lang Vei. On 18 February 1968, the two escaped their captors and Thompson assisted Brande, who was more seriously wounded. Thompson refused Brande's orders to leave him and the two were recaptured. Upon his repatriation in 1973, Thompson was awarded **the Silver Star** for heroism for his actions at Lang Vei and with Brande.

Sergeant Nickloas Fragos, medic, Wounded In Action. Fragos alerted the camp to the tank assault, from his position atop the command bunker. He was later trapped in the command bunker at Lang Vei until the breakout during the afternoon of 7 February 1968. He was later awarded **the Purple Heart** for his actions at Lang Vei. Fragos left the military and became a police officer in Miami. He was **killed in the line of duty** in the late 1970s.

Sergeant Dan Phillips, Missing In Action. Phillips was wounded along with Sergeant William T. Craig as the two defended the western perimeter of the camp with mortar fire. He later escaped through the northern perimeter wire, but became separated from Craig and the others.

Specialist Four William G. McMurray, radio operator, Wounded In Action and **Prisoner Of War**. McMurray was at the Lang Vei camp over a year at the time of the tank battle. Despite his wounds, he continued to communicate with the command bunker, Old Lang Vei, and the artillery at the Khe Sanh Combat Base. He was repatriated in 1973 and is remembered, "as a hard worker and liked by all."

Specialist Four Franklin H. Dooms, radio operator, Wounded In Action. Dooms was the team's primary radio operator during the battle and was trapped in the command bunker until the breakout during the afternoon of 7 February 1968. He was later awarded **the Purple Heart** for his actions at Lang Vei. He is remembered as, "young and enthusiastic," and is believed to be a command sergeant major still on active duty.

MIKE Force Company at Lang Vei

First Lieutenant Paul R. Longgrear, commander, Wounded In Action. Longgrear was trapped in the command bunker until the breakout during the afternoon of 7 February 1968. He was later awarded **the Silver Star, the Vietnamese Cross of Gallantry, Bronze Award, and the Purple Heart** for his actions at Lang Vei. He is remembered as, "a first rate soldier who took good care of his troops." Longgrear later served another tour in Vietnam and several years on active duty. He then became a Christian minister in Georgia. He is also currently a lieutenant colonel in the U.S. Army Reserves.

Sergeant First Class Charles Lindewald, heavy weapons specialist, **Missing In Action**. Lindewald manned the observation point with Sergeant First Class Kenneth Hanna which was overrun

a friend from La Porte, Ind.
a "Wurster's weasel"

early in the battle. Lindewald was wounded early in the battle and is presumed to have died during or shortly after the battle. He is remembered as, "a superb heavy weapons specialist," with six years of Special Forces service at the time of the battle of Lang Vei. He had spent several previous tours in Vietnam and was hand-picked for a "delicate" mission in Laos in 1962.

Sergeant First Class Harvey G. Brande, Wounded In Action and **Prisoner Of War**. Brande was captured with Staff Sergeant Dennis L. Thompson during the battle of Lang Vei. On 18 February 1968, the two escaped their captors and Thompson refused Brande's order to leave him. Upon his repatriation in 1973, Brande was awarded **the Silver Star** for heroism for his actions at Lang Vei and while imprisoned.

Sergeant First Class Earl Burke, Wounded In Action. Burke continued to man the 4.2-inch mortar on the western perimeter of the camp until he ran out of ammunition and was forced to evade through the northern perimeter wire, where he made his way to Old Lang Vei and assisted in the counterattacks of the Lang Vei Camp. He later received **the Purple Heart** for his actions at Lang Vei. He is remembered as, "a solid soldier and a team player."

Sergeant John Early, Wounded In Action. Early was trapped in the command bunker at Lang Vei until the breakout during the afternoon of 7 February 1968. Early later received **the Purple Heart** for his actions at Lang Vei. He is remembered as, "a solid soldier," who later returned to civilian life and became a writer and editor on the staff of *Soldier of Fortune* magazine.

Specialist Four James L. "Wes" Moreland, medic, **Killed In Action**. Moreland was trapped in the command bunker at Lang Vei and received a serious head wound early in the battle. He became delirious and thought that his fellow soldiers in the command bunker were the enemy. He was administered a pain killer to subdue him, which knocked him unconscious. He was barely alive when the breakout from the bunker occurred during the afternoon of 7 February 1968. 1LT Thomas E. Todd found him alone in the bunker before Todd escaped to Old Lang Vei. Todd later reported that Moreland had died.

Lieutenant Colonel Daniel F. Schungel (left) awards Sergeant Richard H. Allen for his valorous actions during the battle of Lang Vei on 7 February 1968.

Photo courtesy of Shelby L. Stanton

Special Forces Team at Old Lang Vei

Lieutenant Colonel Daniel F. Schungel, Wounded In Action. Schungel arrived on site on 6 February 1968 to assist with the Laotian battalion housed at Old Lang Vei. He later organized tank killer teams during the battle of Lang Vei. He miraculously survived his wounds and was later awarded **the Distinguished Service Cross** for his actions at Lang Vei. It is believed he retired from active duty as a brigadier general.

First Lieutenant Thomas E. Todd, engineer officer, Wounded In Action. Todd was at Lang Vei to survey an airstrip at the old camp. He narrowly escaped death during the tank attack and became separated from his fellow soldiers during the night. Todd survived by hiding in the supply bunker until the afternoon of 7 February 1968, when he escaped to Old Lang Vei. Prior to his escape from Lang Vei, Todd went to the command bunker, where he found that Moreland had died. Todd is thought to still be on active duty.

Sergeant First Class Eugene Ashley, medic, **Killed In Action**. Ashley rallied the Laotians at Old Lang Vei for five counterattacks against the tanks at Lang Vei when he realized that the Marines at the Khe Sanh Combat Base would not help. Ashley was posthumously awarded **the Medal of Honor** for his actions at Lang Vei. He is remembered as, "a professional noncommissioned officer who took good care of his troops and exuded a fatherly image."

Sergeant Richard H. Allen, medic, Wounded In Action. Allen assisted Ashley's attempts to counterattack Lang Vei, and later tried to resuscitate Ashley. He was new to Special Forces at the time of the tank battle and was later awarded **the Bronze Star with "V" device for Valor, and the Purple Heart**.

Specialist Four Joel Johnson, medic, Wounded In Action. Johnson assisted Ashley's attempts to counterattack Lang Vei, and also later tried to resuscitate Ashley. Although badly wounded, Johnson continued to assist the evacuation efforts at Old Lang Vei and was later awarded **the Bronze Star with "V" device for Valor, and the Purple Heart**.

14

Remembrances

These remembrances are excerpts taken from a few of the men involved in the story of Lang Vei. They represent some of the more poignant recollections by individuals in and around Khe Sanh. All interviews of the story of Lang Vei have been used in the text and it would have been superfluous to repeat them here.

Paul Longgrear, Lieutenant Colonel (U.S. Army Individual Ready Reserves), then First Lieutenant, Company Commander of the Mobile Strike Force, Lang Vei, during the battle of 1968, where he was trapped in the command bunker:

"I can't tell you the whole story if I don't tell you the whole story:

"When I was separated from the group coming out of the bunker (as they evacuated Lang Vei) I engaged two enemy soldiers who were counting loot from dead bodies. I had paid my Montagnards on 5 February, 196 soldiers, and these two NVA soldiers were counting their money. I became enraged, and turned and engaged them. My ankle, wounded from a hand grenade a little earlier, gave out and I fell; the others thought I'd been shot.

"While I was lying on the ground, time seemed to freeze. The airplanes flying overhead appeared to stop, and everything just halted into dead silence. *Jesus* came to me and said, 'What are you going to do?' Oblivious of everyone and everything else, I had a personal encounter with *the Lord*. I prayed, 'Forgive me, I don't want to die,' and a tremendous peace came over me. Time seemed to start again, airplanes began flying again, the noise started up again.

"With this tremendous peace over me, I slid my rifle behind my back and started down off the hill. I spotted two guys (Special Forces) going down the road. They had heard me shoot and looked to see me flip through the air...they thought I'd been hit.

"We had this understanding that no one would go back for anybody because this was it, this was our last shot. When I joined up with them, they said they thought I'd been hit, but I was so overwhelmed that I didn't know what to tell them.

"Lieutenant Quy, the Vietnamese lieutenant, came driving up in a jeep...the bravest thing I'd ever seen in combat. He left the safety of his camp (Old Lang Vei), drove up in a jeep to where we were, picked us up with three Vietnamese soldiers, and drove right through an enemy ambush. We saw the enemy in the bushes and either the angels were blinding them, or they were so disciplined that they were told not to shoot anything but Marines coming from Khe Sanh...I don't know. But we could see them in the bushes and they watched us drive right through them!"

Allan B. Imes, Lieutenant Colonel, Retired, then captain and commander of the U.S. Army Special Forces team A-728 at Khe Sanh in 1964, two years before it was displaced to Lang Vei:

"I had an outstanding SF 'A' team and I was very proud of them. My memory on names is a little weak, but Sergeant First Class Ronald P. Morris, my intell sergeant, Sergeant First Class Mike Mielke, my weapons sergeant and Sergeant First Class Vic Scaturo, my senior medic, were my mainstays. Mielke was kind of my, 'hero.' A fine warrior from (the) Korean (Conflict), very high professional standards, ramrod straight, a good example for a young officer like myself. In fact, Mielke comes the closest to the 'Rambo' image of anyone I knew in Special Forces!

"Actually, my whole team was excellent and we won our share of praise, with me getting all the credit. Deep down inside I knew then, and know now, I was a very lucky man to get the team I got. We used to laugh because 'old timers' who knew each other pulled strings to get 'picked' and we were formed from the 'leftovers,' so to speak. Yet, we were the best of the lot and I'm sure that can be verified by Major General Dave Watts. Major General Watts (then Major Watts) was the executive officer of the 'B' team at Da Nang...our higher headquarters.

"Our most frightening time was during the Tonkin Bay Crisis. There were supposed to be 20,000 to 30,000 NVA troops ready to attack across the DMZ. I think our government fully expected them to do so, and take as much of I Corps as they could. General John K. Waters, commander of U.S. Army Pacific, came to Khe Sanh to see firsthand the situation for himself. I think he was expecting the attack, also. He gave us our mission if, and when, the attack occurred. Fight initially, but do not try to keep the strike force together. The SF team and Force Recon team (USMC) were to stay behind and conduct guerrilla operations against the NVA. I was to be the Officer-In-Charge of the 'stay behind' forces. There were some uneasy days for a while, to say the least.

"Shortly after that, more and more signs of NVA began to show up. Finally, in late October or early November 1964, one reinforced company from our strike force located a company-sized NVA unit in bivouac northwest of Khe Sanh, in the corner where Laos and Vietnam meet. We surrounded them and in a few minutes shot them up pretty badly. We captured uniform items, German Mauser rifles, etc. We spotted mortars.

"Our problem was keeping the strike force on the objective long enough to search the camp. This was probably the last official spot report I made and to the best of my knowledge, was one of the first confirmed sightings of NVA in South Vietnam. One embarrassing sidelight to that story is that since we only had about one-and-a-half weeks to go (in Vietnam), I sent the Australians (three crackerjack soldiers from the Australian Special Air Service) on this operation. It turned out to be our most successful one. Boy, did they rib us!

"We relied heavily on native rations from time to time. On one occasion, one of our patrols encountered a wild water buffalo. They killed it and brought the meat back to camp. For several days, 'we feasted' on our chunk of meat and bragged about how good it was. All was well, rice and buffalo, until we discovered the meat sitting out, crawling with maggots! Our local *mamasan*, whom we hired to cook for us, just brushed off the maggots, sliced our meat and served it to us with some Vietnamese spices. Needless to say, we kept a closer eye on the kitchen after that!

"Shortly before the Tonkin Crisis, we were getting in a lot of aircraft on our airfield. Hundreds of locals inundated the airstrip for days at a time and virtually threw themselves on the airplanes. I remember one old lady's response when I told the crowd there was nothing I could do for them. She, almost in disbelief, responded that I, 'was a captain in the American Army...I could do anything.' It was my first experience with refugees. Why were they all trying to leave Khe Sanh? One reason was the total isolation of the village from civilization. With the bridges gone, there was virtually no way to get goods, etc., into the area. Another may have been they knew something we didn't know!"

* * *

"Captain Floyd Thompson and I were in the 7th SFG (ABN) out of Fort Bragg. At that time, the 7th Group sent four 'A' teams to Vietnam every six months. Captain Thompson commanded the 'A' team at Khe Sanh prior to my arrival there. He and his men deployed in December 1963 and my 'A' team and I went into pre-mission training at that time.

"We knew that my unit, Detachment A-728 was going to Khe Sanh to replace his team. He became 'Missing In Action' about midway through his tour. He was flying in an L-19 as an observer. One of his missions was to fly over and along the DMZ and Laotian border to spot infiltrating troops and anything out of the ordinary.

"During the last of my pre-mission training days, and upon arrival in Vietnam, all of my briefings along the way included the mission that I try and determine the whereabouts of Captain Floyd Thompson. Thus, on every patrol and operation, indigenous personnel we encountered were questioned as to Thompson's fate.

"It is amazing how many Montagnard tribesmen we questioned who had similar explanations of the airplane that went down and the bodies in it. None, however, could actually pinpoint the exact location. The majority agreed that the two Americans on the aircraft died in the crash. Most of them reported the aircraft was shot down!

"My men and I agreed that the overwhelming response from the people we questioned supported the theory that Captain Floyd Thompson lost his life in Quang Tri Province in 1964, while flying a recon mission along the DMZ and Laotian border.

"Thus, in November 1964 when I made my final after action report, I included the recommendation that Thompson be declared a KIA. You cannot imagine my shock when, in 1973, I was sitting watching the POWs' homecoming on TV and Floyd Thompson was the *second* man off the aircraft!"

Adam Husar, U.S. Army Lieutenant Colonel, Retired, then Major. He was the MIKE Force battalion commander in Da Nang, and commanded the relief force poised at Quang Tri to reinforce the Lang Vei camp:

"I was assigned to I Corps about two weeks before Tet and assumed command of the MIKE Force. I only saw Longgrear a couple of days before he went to Lang Vei with his company to reinforce the camp.

"On the 24th of January, I went up to Lang Vei by helicopter to see my company. I saw the refugees being pushed from Laos toward Khe Sanh by the North Vietnamese. I was wearing regular olive drab fatigues (we didn't wear tiger suits unless we were on a combat operation) and when I saw the refugees coming, all I had was a .45 on the back of my hip. I started walking down through them, asking them questions. I must have gone through several hundred and I started walking into Laos. I heard some shots and I went back to the camp. I told Willoughby, 'We're getting set up for a hit.' To me, it was very obvious. I told Willoughby to put them outside the wire.

"I flew back to Da Nang and told Schungel. The next day I went to USAID and said, 'You've got to get those refugees out of there, they're getting set up for a hit and they have to be dispersed.' Schungel decided to keep a field grade officer up there during this sensitive time and there were only three of us. Hoadley went up there for three or four days and then Schungel relieved him. The morning they got hit, I was supposed to get on the first helicopter out and replace him. It wasn't for diplomatic reasons that he was there, it was for command and control.

"I was asleep that night, probably a little after 12, and they came banging on my door hollering, 'Get up to the TOC!' They got their first message in from Lang Vei and I'm on the radio with Schungel and he says, 'I've got tanks on the CP, send the MIKE Force!' That's it.

"We were in the Tet holidays and I've got a battalion of Chinese Nungs, Rhade and Chieu Hoi, ex-VC. I scrounged about 150 of them, since the holidays were on us. I had two Australians and three other Americans and myself.

We loaded on our trucks and we drove to the Da Nang airbase, not the Marine base. I said, 'I want a C-130 to take us up.' The closest C-130 strip that I could land on was Quang Tri.

"When you go from one base to another, since they're controlled by the Vietnamese and they're paranoid of coups, its hard going on a base with armed troops, especially with my mixture of ethnic groups. We had a hassle, but we finally got on the base and loaded into a C-130 as tight as we could.

"I said, 'I want helicopters to pick us up at Quang Tri and I want to assault right down the chimney, so to speak, on the camp before daybreak, right down on the CP.' We got up to Quang Tri about six o'clock in the morning and sat there all day. We saw helicopters going by us. Two or three o'clock, they sent us back to Da Nang.

"I heard they took a rescue force from FOB-3 and got the survivors out."

William Craig, Command Sergeant Major. Retired, then Sergeant First Class and team sergeant of the Special Forces "A" detachment at Lang Vei during the battle of 1968:

"We offered to send a company of MIKE Force to help them (the U.S. Marines) hold Khe Sanh Village, but the Marines said, no. The Marines said it wasn't worth it, but it was worth it to us because it cut our supply lines to Khe Sanh. If you think picking up air drops is fun, well, we just didn't have the people. We knew we were on our way out when that happened.

"We had one guy named, Holt. We didn't get resupply once for five weeks and lived on noodles the whole time. Anyway, Holt hadn't been married too long and I called the Sergeant Major (at Da Nang) and said, 'We've got some real problems out here.' We had ground fog at Lang Vei that you would not believe, I mean it was so thick you couldn't see three or four feet in front of you. The Sergeant Major came in the next day with a chopper, contour flying, and the fog was so thick, I don't know how he landed. He brought mail and food.

"I think Lang Vei was significant, not only because it was the first time the NVA used tanks, but because it changed the entire structure of I Corps. Because the Marines would not respond to us, I think that's why the Cav (U.S. Army 1st Cavalry Division) was shifted up there. I think (General) Westmoreland decided he didn't want the Marines there. The Marines made contingency plans that they would not follow.

"So they did send the Cav and the Cav went back into Lang Vei. I talked to one guy who went back there and what he described shocked me. The Marines would not go in there, but the Cav did. Here's what they found: 666 bodies that had not been buried and they (the Cav) had never seen that before, never, where the NVA did not bury their dead. They found five burned-out tanks that had not been moved. They found the jeep and Ashley's body, but no other Americans. They said that the area was overgrown, that the natives became superstitious and, I understand, that to this day they won't go up there; knowing the Bru, I believe that.

"As far as fighting the tanks, we had the LAWs, but they were airdropped into the camp before the battle. I don't know if the Army knows this by now, but they should never airdrop LAWs! We were getting about a 90 percent misfire rate...it's not only embarrassing, but we (all) could have lost our lives.

"Before the tank battle and after a firefight near the Sepone River, I sent a young guy down to check the area out. He came back and said, 'I didn't see anything, but I heard some elephants.' I thought, 'Why didn't you tell me that earlier?' The elephants were hauling the NVA dead off, and he said, 'I didn't think it was important.' We had some young people then.

"Before the village at Khe Sanh fell, we used to go up to the combat base in a jeep. Well, one time we needed some parts for our field stove. We had the Bru cook for us, I guess Steptoe had taught them pretty good. Anyway, we went to the mess hall and I asked the mess sergeant for some spare parts and he said, 'No.' I said, 'What do you mean, 'no'?' He told me he had orders not to give the Army anything. So we left the mess hall and the GIs in the chow line were laughing at us as we got in the jeep.

"I was with Lieutenant Bailey and I told Bailey, 'Get out there and lock their goddamn heels,' and if I know Marines, they were still at attention in that chow line the next day. We found some old stove parts, anyway, and that was that.

"They sent a heavy weapons company to Khe Sanh. We knew something was happening (in the area) because we were paying agents all over the place and they know everything that's going on.

"We needed a timing gauge for our 'fifty' (.50 caliber machine gun), so I went to the heavy weapons company to see if I could get one. I found the First Sergeant and he said, 'I'll tell you what I'd like you to do. I'd like you to talk to the company commander.' So I talked to the company commander. I said, 'How long have you been in country?' He said, 'About two weeks.'

"He said if I would answer some questions he'd give me a timing gauge that he'd brought from the states, he'd brought two. He asked me, 'What should I do?' I told him, 'Get commo trenches and get some overhead cover. They have big guns at Co Roc, what're you waiting on?'

"I said, 'Cut those trees down.' He said, 'I can't, the district chief doesn't want us to cut the trees.' I said, 'That son-of-a-bitch is VC, go cut the damn trees down and make up a story. I'd rather be alive and face the district chief than the alternative.'

"You know what? After the whole siege of Khe Sanh, that heavy weapons company came out smelling like a rose. They dug in, something that the rest of the Marines didn't do.

"There were two things blocking Highway 9: Lang Vei and Khe Sanh Village. Khe Sanh Village was in the low ground and you had to occupy the high ground in order to hold it. Lang Vei you could have held forever, I feel. But you need people who will support. When Lang Vei fell, Highway 9 became an Interstate 40.

"They were desperate to take us. They got so desperate once they ran water buffalo through our wire. We ate steak for about a week. They had a couple of sappers with them and we killed them. So I got to thinking about that. That was to see if we had the wire mined. We didn't because there was a restriction against it...we had civilians living inside the camp and it was a hazard to them. But the NVA found out we didn't have any mines."

Thomas Gagnon, USMC Gunnery Sergeant, Retired, then Staff Sergeant and ops chief, 1/13 Field Artillery, at Khe Sang in support of Lang Vei:

"After they hit the (ammo) dump, everything was taken in priority. We only had so many rounds, so they had to be delved out according to the (type of) targets. The FO's of course, were starting to push their targets. They might see one man out there and call in a company, so you have to evaluate each call. So here's a poor guy who's doing his job and he might get overlooked...when I was an FO I did it myself. When I wanted fire I'd do what I had to do to get fire.

"Now, when I'm being shot at I don't want to hear some clown at FDC or FSCC tell me that (the target) is not enough priority. It's a difficult situation.

"That time was so bad. I remember when we were working and some kid got tired (in the Fire Direction Control bunker), he'd crawl under the table and go to sleep and someone would take his place. I was operations chief and when I got tired I'd sit down and the other ops chief would get up. It wasn't a matter of being relieved, it was a matter of having someone there to do the job.

"It was the same way at the guns.

"I was in the FDC the night Lang Vei got hit, we were

on their frequency. They told us, 'tanks are coming through,' and I tell the truth, everybody looked at each other and said, 'Tanks?' We called back and said, 'You'd better re-evaluate,' it could have been anything. Nobody believed there were tanks, nobody. Nobody ever heard of them. We thought they could have confused them with trucks, there was so much going on.

"We decided they were tanks and, of course, fired the artillery. But they (the Special Forces) were out there so far I felt they were sacrificed. Why (did the enemy use) tanks? They had shock value and when you're not ready for them...well, there's not much you can do. And those guys were just stuck out there.

"We weren't too worried because, at Khe Sanh, there was no way they were going to get tanks in on us without us knowing it. We didn't get 'tank fever' at Khe Sanh."

Appendix

PT-76 Amphibious Tank

The Pinquin Arctic tractor chassis, developed in 1948, became the basis for the PT-76 (Piavaiuschiij Tank/Amphibious Tank) in 1952.

The tank's welded hull makes it completely waterproof despite its large size (15.4 tons with a ground clearance of 12 feet). A folding trim vane on the bow, which is extended prior to immersion, and a twin hydrojet propulsion system in the rear of the hull, add to its amphibious qualities. Some PT-76s can also snorkel.

The PT-76's armament includes a 76-millimeter main gun that fires high explosive, armor piercing high explosive, high explosive anti-tank, and high velocity armor piercing rounds. The main gun can sustain a maximum rate of fire of 15 rounds-per-minute with 40 rounds loaded in the ready rack. The main gun can elevate to +30 degrees and can depress to -4 degrees with a 360 degree traverse. A 7.62 millimeter coaxial machine gun completes the tank's armament. There is no anti-aircraft weapon on the tank.

The PT-76 requires a crew of three: tank commander, gunner, and driver. The commander has three episcopes, a white searchlight, and a stadiametrically graduated sight for the coax. The gunner's sight is also stadiametrically graduated with unknown magnification. The driver has three episcopes and can operate the tank's headlights.

The PT-76 operates on a 240-horsepower, water-cooled diesel engine with five forward gears and one reverse gear. Its maximum road speed is 27 miles per hour (six miles-per-hour maximum in the water) and has a maximum road range of 161 miles. The PT-76 can produce smoke through direct injection of diesel fuel into the exhaust system.

The Chinese Communist (People's Republic of China) version of the PT-76, the Type 63, was used by the North Vietnamese Army (NVA) in combat in 1972 and 1975. The Type 63 uses a slightly different turret design and has an 85-millimeter main gun.

The PT-76's thin skin, which enhances its waterborne capabilities, also makes it vulnerable to small arms fire.

Inventive NVA tankers attached rubber matting, wire mesh, and

ARVN soldiers pose with a Soviet-made PT-76 amphibious tank captured from the NVA in a 1971 raid in the southern panhandle of Laos. PT-76s were first used by the NVA at the battle of the Lang Vei Special Forces "A" camp on 7 February 1968. Note the field-expedient shields emplaced on the hull and turret of the tank by the NVA. These shields were used to deflect or prematurely detonate anti-tank rounds. This technique was also used by US tank crewmen.

Photo courtesy of the US Military History Institute

This burned-out, Soviet-made PT-76 tank is examined the morning after the enemy failed to over-run the Ben Het Special Forces camp in May 1969. Several PT-76s were destroyed in that battle by US tanks in the only armor-versus-armor engagement of the war. Similar tanks were first used by the NVA in the attack on the Lang Vei Special Forces camp 7 February 1968.

Photo courtesy of the US Military History Institute

178

This aerial view of a mainland Chinese Type 63 tank was taken in 1972 during the Easter offensive effort by the communists. Type 63 tanks were used by the North Vietnamese Army and were often reported as PT-76s, with which they are identical except for minor modifications.

Photo courtesy of the U.S. Military History Institute

wheel drums to the outside of the turrets to deflect or to prematurely detonate incoming rounds, in an effort to make the tank more survivable. Its primary mission is reconnaissance and not heavy combat.

The Soviet Union exports the PT-76 to its allies, which include Angola, Bulgaria, Cuba, Finland, East Germany, Hungary, Laos, North Korea, Syria, Yugoslavia, and the Socialist Republic of Vietnam.

The Soviet Union has also provided dozens of PT-76s to Nicaragua.

Author's Notes

FOREWORD

1. MacArthur, Douglas A., General, U.S.A. Annual Report of the Chief of Staff for the Fiscal Year Ending June 30, 1935, Washington, D.C.

2. Summers, Harry G. Jr., *On Strategy: A Critical Analysis of the Vietnam War*, Presidio Press, Novato, California, 1982.

3. Luttwak, Edward N., *The Pentagon and the Art of War*, Simon and Schuster, New York, 1984, page 151.

4. Field Manual 100-5: Operations of Army Forces in the Field, Washington, D.C.: September 1968.

PART I

CHAPTER 1. "TANKS IN THE WIRE!"

Several excellent sources exist on the battle of Lang Vei. Among them: the official US Army after action report (AAR) on file with the Military History Institute at Carlisle Barracks, PA; an account in *Seven Firefights in Vietnam* by John A. Cash; the US Air Force participation in the battle as explained by Bernard C. Nalty in *Air Power and the Fight for Khe Sanh*; *The Battle for Khe Sanh* by US Marine Corps Captain Moyers S. Shore II on file with the USMC History and Museums Division; and Shelby Stanton's *The Rise and Fall of an American Army* and *Green Berets at War*.

The AAR is the basis for Cash's narrative and the other two accounts reflect the Air Force and Marine Corps point of the view, respectively.

One other good account of Lang Vei is in *The End of the Line: The Siege of Khe Sanh* by Robert Pisor. His book features Lang Vei as one of several "Bitter Little Battles" in the Khe Sanh area and is derived from the above mentioned sources. It is Pisor's well-researched and vividly written style that is so engaging.

Finally, there are the interviews. The primary interview in the first chapter is with Paul R. Longgrear, the MIKE Force company commander at Lang Vei during the 1968 battle.

"Hello lieutenant...": Longgrear interview.

The women and children with the Lao battalion: Pisor, *The End of the Line*, p. 113.

"Where are your casualties?": Longgrear interview.

Later on the 24th...: Longgrear interview and AAR, p. 6.

8,000 noncombatants: Cash, *Seven Firefights*, p. 111.

Du surrenders: Longgrear interview; Pisor, p. 166; and AAR, p. 6.

"...the world's best actor...": Longgrear interview.

Patrol discovers a road: Pisor, p. 166 and AAR p. 6.

Willoughby suspected...: AAR, p. 30.

Defenses at Lang Vei were improved: Pisor, p. 167 and AAR p. 6.

Bunkers had been reinforced: Pisor, p. 76.

Weapons in the Lang Vei camp: Cash, p. 113 and 117.

MIKE Force OP spooked by shadows: Longgrear interview.

Forty-two minutes after midnight: Pisor, p. 168.

CHAPTER 2. "A DIRTY, DISGUSTING WAR":
THE AMERICANS TAKE CHARGE

The interviews used for this chapter were: U.S. Army LTC (Ret.) Allan B. Imes, former "A" team commander at the Special Forces camp at Khe Sanh 1964; former U.S. Army First Lieutenant Mike Perkins, then the executive officer of the Special Forces camp at Lang Vei/Khe Sanh in 1966; former U.S. Army Sergeant First Class Bill Steptoe, team sergeant and survivor of the 1967 battle of Lang Vei; U.S. Army MAJ (Ret.) James Whitenack, advisory chief in Khe Sanh Village 1967; U.S. Army Staff Sergeant Thomas Veneziani, a helicopter door gunner with the 161st Aviation Company in Hue/Phu Bai 1967;

and with my father, U.S. Army LTC (Ret.) Harvey L. Stockwell, an engineer advisor in Hue 1960-61.

Poilane and other background data on Khe Sanh: Pisor, chapter three.

"A" Team establishes Khe Sanh outpost: Stanton, *Green Berets at War,* p. 86, and Pisor, p. 70.

CIDG program: Simpson, *Inside the Green Berets,* p. 97-98.

"...a dirty, disgusting...": Fall, *Street Without Joy,* p. 244.

East-west, all-weather road: Cash, p. 110.

Captain Floyd Thompson and Khe Sanh 1964: Imes interview.

Anti government protests: Pisor, p. 71.

"...tactics and weapons...": Herr, *Dispatches,* p. 119.

U.S. losses at Ia Drang Valley: Herr p. 100.

Westmoreland's briefings: Imes interview.

"Khe Sanh could serve...": Westmoreland, *Reports,* p. 336.

Description of Khe Sanh 1966: Perkins interview.

"This was beautiful...": *Chaplains with Marines in Vietnam,* p. 120.

The runway, "Fort Dix," the bombing of Lang Vei Village, and "setting out honey to attract flies": Pisor, p. 73-74, and Perkins interview.

U.S. Army advisory team in Khe Sanh Village: Whitenack interview.

Hill Fights: Shore, p. 10.

M-16 rifle malfunctions: Pisor, p. 6.

"...outstanding camouflage...": Pisor, p. 74.

Crenshaw and Stallings: Steptoe interview.

Enemy situation during Hill Fights: Pisor, p. 74.

Lang Vei camp overrun: Whitenack and Steptoe interviews.

Classic adaptation of infiltration: Kelley, *U.S. Army Special Forces, 1961-71,* p. 110.

Lang Vei rebuilt: Pisor, p. 75.

Codewords: Clarke interview.

"...wretches...": Pisor, p. 76.

Marines stumbled about...: Pisor, p. 73.

Relief rehearsal took 19 hours: Shore, p. 67.

...feared the Marines...: Pisor, p. 76.

Reported areas clear: Longgrear interview.

Artillery convoy: Pisor, p. 75.

Helicopter vs. tank: Veneziani interview.

MIKE Force moves to Lang Vei: Longgrear interview.

Relief force poised at Khe Sanh: Shore, p. 67.

CHAPTER 3. THE "YARDS"—MOUNTAIN FIGHTERS

The plight of the Montagnards is deceptive. To the Westerner's view, it is too easy to claim that the differences between Montagnards and Vietnamese, or between Montagnard tribes, were "cultural" or "political." One Montagnard living in the United States, whom I will refer to as Han, was a GVN official for Montagnard affirmative action and granted me an interview. He took exception to these publicized differences, but his explanation perplexed me. Suffice to say that portions of his interview used in the text may be a bit oversimplified.

Other interviews with Duc and Van, Vietnamese friends of mine, provided insight into the history of their former country. I am indebted to them for their patience with me and I am impressed with their patriotism toward America.

Duc and I searched through Vietnamese book stores in downtown Sacramento (CA) for accounts of Lang Vei, and he helped translate some fine sources for me.

In my search for Vietnamese and Montagnards to interview I learned that many did not want to talk for fear their names may become known to the present regime in Vietnam and their family members still in that country may suffer.

I am not smitten with enough grandeur to think that my meager book may cause someone harm so far away, and those to whom I spoke did not mind their names being used. I chose, however, to identify them only by their first names out of mutual respect and for my own peace of mind.

800,000 to one million: Pike, *Viet Cong,* p. 13.

Montagnard lifestyle: Sochurek, "Vietnam's Montagnards,": p. 445 and p. 447.

U.S. Army captain parachutes into the highlands: Sochurek, "Vietnam's Montagnards," p. 444.

Ho receives American aid: Bouscaren, *Diem of Vietnam,* p. 18-19.

"...presence of American senior officers...": Bouscaren, p. 19.

Villages as sanctuaries: Sochurek, "Vietnam's Montagnards," p. 444.

Ownership of land: interview.

"...free people...": interview.

"They can cross...": interview.

"...outsiders would protect us...": interview.

Military school in Soa Cam: interview.

Former captive Special Forces sergeant returns to Montagnards: Sochurek, "Vietnam's Montagnards," p. 443.

Relationship between Viet Cong and Montagnards: Pike, *Viet Cong,* p. 250.

Montagnard affairs office: Han interview.

Viet Cong assassinate chieftain of Khe Sanh Village: Han interview.

Shift to Ministry of Defense: Han interview.

FULRO: Han interview, and Westmoreland, p. 78.

"Diem's head...": Bouscaren, p. 97.

Diem ends 500-year tradition: Fall, *Last Reflections,* p. 233.

Government officials kidnaped: Bouscaren, p. 163.

"Robin Hood halo": Fall, *Last Reflections,* p. 234.

Soa Cam trains VNSF: Han interview.

Montagnard revolt: Sochurek, "Americans in Action in Vietnam," p. 38-65.

"...look at their tin huts...": Han interview.

CHAPTER 4. "VOLCANO UNDER THE SNOW"—THE ENEMY

The intention of this chapter is to provide some insight into the North Vietnamese Army's tactics in order to better understand its first use of tanks against Americans forces. That insight, though, is elusive.

Several books by Giap have been translated into English, but most of them are compilations of propaganda press releases fed to the Vietnamese people throughout the years. *How We Won the War* is the translation that best provides an "inside look" at the NVA, but it is more strategy oriented rather than tactical. Giap's discussion of strategy here is based on the successful seizure of South Vietnam by the North in 1975. Giap does not discuss losses.

Viet Cong, by Douglas Pike is a remarkably thorough look at the guerrilla leaders and fighters in South Vietnam, as well as a look at the history of the country's struggle against foreign occupation. These guerrillas were the backbone of the "freedom struggle," and it is interesting to note that Giap ignores their contributions in *How We Won*, but rather he pontificates on the use of conventional warfare in 1975 to unify Vietnam.

Finally, in a longshot attempt to get direct input from the Vietnamese, I wrote letters to General Giap and the Vietnamese Defense Ministry. I sent letters a second time, on this occasion through the Vietnamese ambassador to the United Nations in New York, and through the Australian ambassador to the Socialist Republic of Vietnam in Hanoi. My letters went unanswered and were never returned.

Giap was born...: Giap, *People's War, People's Army* (biographical foreward on Giap by Bernard Fall), p. xxix.

Chinese invade Vietnam: Fall foreward, p. xxix-xxxii.

Background on Giap: Fall foreward, P. xxix-xxxii.

"...half starved Santa Claus...": Fall, *Last Reflections,* p. 59.

Ho's aliases: Pike, p. 10.

"Volcano Under the Snow": Fall foreward, p. xxxiii.

Law degree: Fall foreward, p. xxix.

34-man unit: Fall foreward, p. xxxiv.

Giap's battlefield losses: Pisor, p. 136.

Battle of Dien Bien Phu: Pisor, p. 137.

Composition of French force: Fall, *Street,* p. 327.

North Vietnamese coolies: Fall, Hell, p. 452. 18th century siege technique: Fall, *Street,* p. 324.

Giap's writing are studied: Pisor, p. 125.

"Time...": Pisor, p. 127.

Marshal Tran Hung Dao: Fall, *Last Reflections,* p. 41.

"Surprise...": Giap, *How We Won,* p. 53-54.

GM 100: Davis, "Legions in the Sky," p. 48-49.

2,000 graves filled with lime: Davis, p. 48.

Growth of NVA: Van Dyke, *North Vietnam's Strategy for Survival,* p. 111.

Politics and the NVA: Van Dyke, p. 111.

"For Nation—Forget Self": Pisor, p. 144.

Soldier's pay is sent home: Van Dyke, p. 112.

"Revolutionary ethics...": Van Dyke, p. 116.

"Three-man cell": Van Dyke, p. 119.

Political commissars: Van Dyke, p. 117.

Giap monitors morale: Fall, *Street,* p. 34.

U.S. overestimates itself: Pisor, p. 140.

"...unshakable conviction...": Pisor, p. 144.

"Every Citizen...": Van Dyke, p. 123.

...every manual: Pisor, p. 142.

Truck drivers: Van Dyke, p. 53.

U.S. bombing efforts peak: Van Dyke, p. 40.

Destructors: Van Dyke, p. 54.

Dac cong: Pisor, p. 142. (The North Vietnamese refer to their commandos as biet kich. Dac cong is not an inexact term, but it was used by the South Vietnamese to denigrate their enemies.)

Giap's strategy: Pearson, *War in the Northern Provinces,* p. 93-95.

Special Forces camps become targets: Pearson, p. 6-8.

NVA strength in South Vietnam: Pearson, p. 7.

Sophisticated equipment: Pearson, p. 8.

Militant Buddhists: Pearson, p.8.

U.S. interpretation of enemy strategy: Pearson, p. 93-95.

"Our strategy...": Fall, *Street,* p. 35.

Giap plans Tet: Pisor, p. 145.

Giap's conclusions: Pearson, p. 93-95.

CHAPTER 5. THE TET OFFENSIVE

Tet!, by Don Oberdorfer, *Big Story,* by Peter Braestrup, and *War in the Northern Provinces,* by Lieutenant General Willard Pearson provided this overview of the communist general offensive in 1968. Especially enlightening was Robert Pisor's, *The End of the Line: The Siege of Khe Sanh.* His treatment of those sources was complimented by his personal notes, written while he covered Tet as a Vietnam correspondent.

"...historic campaign...": Oberdorfer, *Tet!,* p. 117.

JUSPAO: Oberdorfer, p. 116.

67,000 NVA: Oberdorfer, p. 116.

NVA hopes: Oberdorfer, p. 117.

All-out offensive unlikely: Oberdorfer, p.120.

U.S. command reducing: Oberdorfer, p. 120.

Difference of opinions: Oberdorfer, p. 121.

"If we'd gotten...": Oberdorfer, p. 121.

USS Pueblo: Oberdorfer, p. 111.

Theory on Pueblo attack: Oberdorfer, p. 163.

Massive concentrations: Pisor, p. 122.

NVA command net silenced: Oberdorfer, p. 110-111. Nalty, in *Airpower and the Fight for Khe Sanh,* called this bombardment the largest U.S. airstrike of the war, p. 82.

"...boogey man...": Fallaci, *Interview with History,* p. 74.

Tet customs: White/Garret, "South Vietnam Fights the Red Tide," p. 445.

Nha Trang and other cities: Oberdorfer, p. 121-124.

Alpha Troop, 2-1 Cav: Department of the Army Lineage and Honors.

Tet truce canceled: Oberdorfer, p. 133.

Saigon: Oberdorfer, p. 134-136 and p. 141-142.

Viet Cong sapper team: Pisor, p. 150.

Thirty-six paratroopers: Pisor, p. 150.

Hue: Oberdorfer, p. 198-201.

White House: Pisor, p. 150.

CHAPTER 6. STRATEGY AND THE MEDIA

When I included some notes on the media and Vietnam in a rough draft of this manuscript to Colonel Bruce B.G. Clarke, he wrote back, "Whole books need to be written about this!" He was right.

The treatment of that subject here admittedly barely scratches the surface, yet it deserves attention. The relationship between the combat soldier and news correspondents (in the first war that America's journalists experienced virtually total freedom of coverage) is best summed up in a true story about Lang Vei's survivors.

Jim Morris, a Special Forces officer who alternated between "A" team duty and a Public Information Officer (PIO) post, describes a press conference for the Lang Vei survivors in his book, *War Story*:

"...I got to a Marine PIO colonel and suggested that we hold a press conference for those Lang Vei survivors who wanted to appear. Four of the Lang Vei survivors came over to the press camp and were interviewed on all three TV networks and all the wire services and news magazines. I wasn't too happy about their being scrubbed and put into baggy fatigues with the supply-room smell on them. I'd have been happier to have them in tiger suits and bandages.

"There was no question about it. We had the shit kicked out of us at Lang Vei, but those guys were so cool at their press conference, and it was obvious they had fought so bravely when outnumbered so badly, that I like to think we turned our military defeat into a psychological victory. My own little 'Tet Offensive' within a Tet Offensive."

Few correspondents went beyond the "supply-room smell" and actually acknowledged the Green Berets' accomplishments. Michael Herr was one who did. He wrote in his book, *Dispatches*:

"During the early morning of February 7, something so horrible happened in the Khe Sanh sector that even those of us who were in Hue when we heard news of it had to relinquish our own fear and despair for a moment to acknowledge the horror and pay some tribute to it. It was as though the very worst dream any of us had ever had about the war had come true; it anticipated nightmares so vile that they could take you off shuddering in your sleep. No one who heard it was able to smile that bitter, secret survivor's smile that was the reflex to almost all news of disaster. It was too awful even for that...

"The Marines at Khe Sanh saw the Lang Vei survivors come in. They saw them and heard about them up in their Special Forces compound, holding off all visitors at rifle point, saw their faces and their unfocused stares, and they talked quietly among themselves about it. Jesus, they had tanks. Tanks!..."

...clear to Westmoreland: Pearson, p. 93-95.

"...about to run out of steam...": Pisor, p. 152.

Television war: Oberdorfer, p. 159.

"...lies within our grasp...": Oberdorfer, p. 128 (d) under photos.

TV and newspaper reports: Oberdorfer, p. 331.

Stalemate and mistake: Oberdorfer, p. 161.

CHAPTER 7. THE SIEGE OF KHE SANH

While Robert Pisor's book is the most comprehensive study of the siege, USMC Captain Moyers S. Shore II painstakingly wrote, *The Battle for Khe Sanh*, for the Marine Corps History and Museums

Division. Shore's work was produced under Marine and Army scrutiny, and while it is reportedly flawed by the many official approvals it required to be published, he collected the views and notes of every significant individual in the battle.

Interviews conducted for this chapter were with Longgrear, and U.S. Army Colonel Bruce B.G. Clarke, who was the advisory commander in Khe Sanh Village when it was abandoned.

NVA officers killed outside perimeter: Shore, p. 30.

Situation map updated: Pisor, p. 83.

Tiger in the perimeter trash pit: Gagnon interview.

"Niagra": Shore, p. 94.

Men of India Company: Shore, p. 31.

Kilo Company: Shore, p. 31.

2d Battalion/26th Regiment arrives: Shore, p. 31.

First time since Iwo Jima: Shore, p. 30-31.

Fire support plan: Shore, p. 32-3.

"...like a page out of Chesty Puller's life...": Shore, p. 35.

Tonc surrenders: Shore, p. 39.

Tonc details Tet: Shore, p. 39.

Enemy attacks as planned: Shore, P. 39-41.

Gunners sing Marine Corps Hymn: Shore, p. 41.

Chain of explosions: Shore, p. 42-43.

Clouds of tear gas: Shore, p. 43.

Khe Sanh Village advisory group: Pisor, p. 97 and Clarke interview.

Marines evacuate Khe Sanh Village: Clarke and Longgrear interviews.

"Experts" critical of Khe Sanh stand: Shore, p. 45.

Westmoreland studies Dien Bien Phu: Westmoreland, p. 337-338.

Nuclear weapons: Pisor, p. 153-4.

COFRAM: Oberdorfer, p. 186.

...no Dien Bien Phu...: Pisor, p. 122.

PART II

CHAPTER 8. CALLSIGN, "JACKSONVILLE"

It's impossible to realize the terrible, daily strain of the Marines at Khe Sanh. Tom Gagnon, the former USMC staff sergeant and one of the artillery operations chiefs at Khe Sanh, provided a personal glimpse of the dust and emotions of life at the combat base.

Feels the dread: Gagnon interview.

Incoming artillery compared to Second World War: Pisor, p.194.

Persistence of enemy artillery fire: Pisor, p. 194-195.

"Indian Country": Gagnon interview.

Gave Bernard Fall the title of his book: Pisor, p. 137.

Green Berets greet Marine forward observer: Longgrear interview.

Callsign, "Jacksonville": Craig interview.

Incoming artillery rounds sound like outgoing: Herr, *Dispatches,* p. 132.

Wasn't funny anymore: Gagnon interview.

CHAPTER 9. LONGGREAR'S "YARDS"

Paul Longgrear provided the majority of information used in this chapter through interviews.

MIKE Force: Longgrear interview.

Hre felt snubbed: Longgrear interview.

Mobile Guerrilla Force: Early, "Armor in the Wire," p. 72.

"...love-hate affair...": Longgrear interview.

CHAPTER 10. COUNTDOWN TO THE BATTLE

Advisory group established after mistaken bombing: Whitenack interview.

"Howard Johnson's": Pisor, p. 79. and Clarke interview.

"Protection money": Imes interview.

Special Forces offers MIKE Force company to reinforce ville: Craig interview.

Americans and Regional Force have to walk to combat base: Clarke interview.

Hid weapons in pajamas: Longgrear interview.

Cry for help: Pisor, p. 105-106.

Heliborne raid: Clarke interview.

Bombers can't find tanks: Pisor, p. 106.

33d Royal Laotian Elephant Battalion: Longgrear and Husar interviews.

Lack of credibility: Longgrear interview.

Contingent arrives to assist Laotians: Cash, p. 111-112.

Du surrenders: Longgrear interview.

Young captured: Grant, *Survivors*, p. 189-195.

MIKE Force ambush of NVA: unclassified teletype message from Colonel Ladd, commander of all Special Forces in Vietnam, to A-101 offering congratulations to the soldiers.

Hres brought into camp: Longgrear interview.

Schungel replaces Hoadley in camp: Husar interview.

Incoming artillery rounds impact at Lang Vei camp: AAR, p. 2.

"Many...many VC": Longgrear interview.

Camp and OP open fire: AAR, p. 31.

Young interrogated: Grant, p. 196-197.

"Would you like to watch us...?": Grant, p. 197.

"Why don't they...?": Cash, p. 119.

CHAPTER 11. THE BATTLE OF LANG VEI

"I've got five tanks...": Early, p. 74.

LAWs misfire, fail to penetrate enemy armor: Longgrear interview.

Tank killer teams organized: AAR, p. 7, and Longgrear interview.

"Jacksonville, Jacksonville, this is Spunky Hansen": Early, p. 74.

"We've got a few...": Longgrear interview.

Todd: AAR, p. 13.

Marines at Khe Sanh receive barrage: Gagnon interview.

Craig and Phillips: Craig interview and his after action report, not filed with the official compilation. His report was taken as an officially sworn statement while he was recovering from his wounds at the Camp Kue U.S. Army hospital on Okinawa.

Holt: AAR, p. 14-15.

Harrington: Nalty, p. 33.

Field artillery Digital Automatic Computer: Gagnon interview.

Quy captured: Schungel letter.

OP reports it is surrounded: Early, p. 76.

Fresh bandages visible on NVA soldiers: Early, p. 76.

15 secondary explosions: Nalty, p. 33-34.

✓ "Charlie's been hit in the gut...!": Early, p. 76.

Schungel and Wilkins: Longgrear interview and AAR, p. 7-8.

"Help us!": Early, p. 76.

Westmoreland won't second guess commanders in the field: Westmoreland, p. 341.

Relief troops in Da Nang are rallied: Husar interview.

Ashley assists camp: AAR, p. 35-36.

Lao battalion commander refuses to help: Early, p. 76.

Moreland becomes violent and is injected with morphine: Longgrear interview.

VNSF in bunker surrender: AAR, p. 35.

Americans in bunker await assault, explosions rip through walls: Long-grear interview.

"It's no good...": Early, p. 76.

Schungel and Wilkins: AAR, p. 7-8.

Westmoreland issues orders from Da Nang: Oberdorfer, p. 189-190.

Entombed Americans plan escape: Longgrear interview.

Dog tags and ID cards are buried and destroyed: Longgrear interview. Longgrear speculated that the NVA often took these items from dead Americans during the war and claimed they were prisoners to inflate POW figures for political reasons. This speculation received some verification in media reports in late 1985 regarding American-Vietnamese discussion on MIAs.

Moreland left behind: Longgrear interview.

"...the bravest thing...": Longgrear interview.

Helicopters arrive at Old Lang Vei: Longgrear interview.

Todd: AAR, p. 13.

Americans arrive at Khe Sanh from Lang Vei: Longgrear interview.

CHAPTER 12. AFTER ACTION REPORT

Statistics: AAR, p. 5.

Notes and recommendations: AAR, p. 4-5.

Summary and 1/26 logbook: Pisor, p. 175.

USMC film: "Vietnam Remember."

Marines prepare for attacks: Pisor, p. 176.

"After Lang Vei...": Herr, p. 120.

Correspondence sent home: Gagnon interview.

Operation Pegasus: Pisor, p. 216 and 220-223.

"One of the reasons...": Thompson, *No Exit*, p. 68-69.

"There were two enemy divisions...": Westmoreland, p. 339.

"Dien Bien Phu...": Fallaci, p. 85.

"North Vietnam says...": Braestrup, *Big Story*, p. 488.

Hue: Oberdorfer, p. 197-235.

Tet boomerangs American support of the war: Oberdorfer, p. 170-177.

Lang Vei controversies, AAR and Grant, *Survivors*, p. 189 and 196-197.

MIKE Force not used to relieve camp: Husar interview.

Theory on why tanks were used: Pisor personal letter.

Major Quamo: Stanton, *Green Berets*, p. 161.

Quy, Thompson, and Brande: Longgrear interview.

Gagnon letter and interview with his mother.

Fate of Bru: Simpson, p. 111-112, and Han interview.

Published letter from Colonel Jackson: *Delta Digest*.

CHAPTER 13. ROLL CALL/AWARDS AND DECORATIONS

This chapter was compiled from official orders and remembrances from some of the participants of the battle of Lang Vei.

The orders on all awards given to members of the battle are incomplete. I included only those awards that I can verify, but where members are not credited with specific awards, I believe that they received either a Silver Star, Bronze Star with "V" device for valor, or a Bronze Star.

I regret discrepancies caused by a lack of official awards orders.

CHAPTER 14. REMEMBRANCES

These excerpts were taken from some of the personal interviews I conducted.

PT-76 Amphibious Tank

Information used in the appendix came from *Modern Armor: A Comprehensive Guide* by Squadron Signal Publications, 1978.

Bibliography

Baker, Mark. *Nam*. New York: Berkley Books, 1983.

Brende, Joel Osler and Parson, Erwin Randolph. *Vietnam Veterans: The Road to Recovery*. New York and London: Plenum Press, 1985.

Bouscaren, Anthony T. *Diem of Vietnam*. Pittsburgh, PA: Duquesne University Press, 1965.

Braestrup, Peter. *Big Story: How the American Press and Television Reported and Interpreted the Crisis in Vietnam and Washington*. Garden City, NY: Anchor Press/Doubleday, 1978.

Caputo, Philip. *A Rumor of War*. Toronto: Holt, Rinehart and Winston, 1977.

Dawson, Alan. *55 Days: The Fall of South Vietnam*. New Jersey: Prentice-Hall, Inc. 1977.

Del Vecchio, John M. *The 13th Valley*. New York: Bantam Books, 1982.

Donlon, Captain Roger H.C. and Rogers, Warren. *Outpost of Freedom*. New York: McGraw-Hill Book Company, 1965.

Dougan, Clark and Weiss, Stephen. *Nineteen Sixty Eight: The Vietnam Experience*. Boston: Boston Publishing Company, 1983.

Downs, Frederick. *Aftermath*. New York, W.W. Norton, 1984.
—*The Killing Zone*. New York: Berkley Books, 1983.

Dunstan, Simon. *Vietnam Tracks: Armor in Battle 1945-75*. Novato, CA: Presidio Press, 1982.

Edelman, Bernard (editor). *Dear America: Letters Home from Vietnam*. New York and London: W.W. Norton and Company, 1985.

Eilert, Rick. *For Self and Country*. New York: William Morrow and Company, 1983.

Fall, Bernard B. *Hell in a Very Small Place: The Seige of Dien Bien Phu*. New York: Vintage Books, 1968.
—*Last Reflections on a War*. Garden City, NY: Doubleday and Company, 1967.
—*Street Without Joy*. Harrisburg, PA: The Stackpole Company, 1964.

—*The Two Vietnams* (revised edition). New York: Frederick A. Praeger, 1966.

Fallaci, Oriana. *Interview with History.* New York: Liveright Publishing Corporation, 1976.

Fitzgerald, Frances. *Fire in the Lake.* Boston: Little, Brown and Company, 1972.

Fuller, Jack. *Fragments.* New York: William Morrow and Company, 1984.

Giap, Vo Nguyen. *Big Victory, Great Task.* New York: Frederick A. Praeger, 1968.

—*How We Won the War.* Ypsilanti, MI: Recon Publications, 1976.

—*People's War, People's Army.* Hanoi: Foreign Language Publishing House, 1974.

Glasser, Ronald J. *365 Days.* New York: Bantam Books, 1971.

—*Another War, Another Peace.* New York: Ballantine Books, 1985.

Goldman, Peter L. *Charlie Company: What Vietnam Did to Us.* New York: William Morrow and Company, 1983.

Grant, Zalin. *Survivors: American POWs in Vietnam.* New York: Berkley Books, 1985.

Groom, Winston and Spencer, Duncan. *Conversations with the Enemy: The Story of PFC Robert Garwood.* New York: G.P. Putnam's Sons, 1983.

Herbert, Anthony B. with Wooten, James T. *Soldier.* New York: Dell Publishing Company, 1973.

Herr, Michael. *Dispatches.* New York: Alfred A. Knopf, 1977.

Hubbell, John G. *POW.* Pleasantville, NY: Reader's Digest Press, 1977.

Karnow, Stanley. *Vietnam: A History.* New York: The Viking Press, 1983.

Kovic, Ron. *Born on the Fourth of July.* New York: McGraw-Hill Book Company, 1976.

Kukler, Michael A. *Operation Barooom.* Gastonia, NC: Self published, 1985.

Mason, Robert L. *Chickenhawk.* New York: The Viking Press, 1983.

Maclear, Michael. *The Ten Thousand Day War: Vietnam 1945-75.* New York: Avon Books, 1981.

McDonough, Lieutenant Colonel James R. *Platoon Leader.* Novato, CA: Presidio Press, 1985.

Morris, Jim. *War Story.* New York: Dell Publishing, 1985.

Oberdorfer, Don. *Tet!* Garden City, NY: Doubleday and Company, 1971.

O'Brien, Tim. *If I Die in a Combat Zone.* New York: Delacorte Press, 1973.

Page, Tim. *Tim Page's Nam.* New York: Alfred A. Knopf, 1983.

Pickerell, James. *Vietnam in the Mud.* Indianapolis, New York, and Kansas City: The Bobbs-Merrill Company, Inc., 1966.

Pike, Douglas. *Viet Cong.* Cambridge, MA: The M.I.T. Press, 1966.

Pisor, Robert. *The End of the Line: The Siege of Khe Sanh.* New York: Ballantine Books, 1982.

Rowe, James N. *Five Years to Freedom.* Boston, Toronto: Little, Brown and Company, 1971.

Roy, Jules. *Battle of Dien Bien Phu.* New York: Pyramid Books, 1966.

Santoli, Albert. *Everything We Had.* New York: Random House, 1981.

Scott, Lieutenant Colonel Leonard B. *Charlie Mike.* New York: Ballantine Books, 1985.

Simpson, Colonel Charles M. III. *Inside the Green Berets.* Novato, CA: Presidio Press, 1983.

Squadron Signal Publications. *Modern Armor: A Comprehensive Guide,* 1978.

Stanton, Shelby L. *The Rise and Fall of an American Army: US Ground Forces in Vietnam, 1965-73.* Novato, CA: Presidio Press, 1985.

—*Green Berets at War: US Army Special Forces in Southeast Asia 1956-75.* Novato, CA: Presidio Press, 1985.

Summers, Colonel Harry G. Jr. *On Strategy: A Critical Analysis of the Vietnam War.* Novato, CA: Presidio Press, 1982.

Terry, Wallace. *Bloods: An Oral History of the Vietnam War by Black Veterans.* New York: Random House, 1984.

Thompson, Sir Robert. *No Exit from Vietnam.* New York: David McKay Company, 1969.

Van Dyke, Jon M. *North Vietnam's Strategy for Survival.* Palo Alto, CA: Pacific Books, 1972.

Webb, James H. Jr. *Fields of Fire.* Englewood Cliffs, NJ: Prentice-Hall, 1978.
—*A Sense of Honor.* New York: Bantam Books, 1982.

West, F.J. Jr. *The Village.* New York: Harper & Row, 1972.

Westmoreland, General William C. *A Soldier Reports.* Garden City, NY: Doubleday and Company, 1976.

Wheeler, John. *Touched with Fire: The Future of the Vietnam Generation.* New York: Avon Books, 1985.

SELECTED ARTICLES

Andrade, Dale. "The NVA Surprise," *Soldier of Fortune*, February, 1985.

Cossey, CPT Gerald R. "Tank vs. Tank," *Armor: The Magazine of Mobile Warfare*, September-October, 1970.

Davis, James M. "Legion in the Clouds," *Frontiers*, May, 1985.

Delta Digest. "Customer Service Citation," August, 1968.

Early, CPT John. "Armor in the Wire: MACV Vacillates During Lang Vei Slaughter," *Soldier of Fortune*, November, 1979.

Greenman, Ronald. "Long Night at Lang Vei," *Soldier of Fortune*, February, 1985.

Nalty, Bernard C. "Khe Sanh: No Dien Bien Phu," *Soldier of Fortune*, May, 1980.

Newsweek. "How the US Lost Lang Vei," February 19, 1968.

Sochurek, Howard. "Air Rescue Behind Enemy Lines," *National Geographic*, September, 1968.
—"Americans in Action in Vietnam," *National Geographic*, January, 1965.

—"Slow Train Through Vietnam's War," *National Geographic*, September, 1964.

—"Vietnam's Montagnards," *National Geographic*, April, 1968.

White, Peter T. "Behind the Headlines in Vietnam," *National Geographic*, February, 1967.

White, Peter T. and Garrett, W.E. "The Mekong: River of Terror and Hope," *National Geographic*, December, 1968.

—"South Vietnam Fights the Red Tide," *National Geographic*, October, 1961.

MILITARY AND GOVERNMENT SOURCES

After Actions Report, Lang Vei. Military History Institute, Carlisle Barracks, PA. March 1968.

Albright, John; Cash, John A.; and Sandstrum, Allan W. *Seven Firefights in Vietnam*. Office of the Chief of Military History, US Army, Washington, DC, 1970.

ARVN General Staff. *Cuoc Tong Cong Kich—Tong Khoi Nghia Cua Viet Cong (The Tet Offensive)*. Reprinted by Dai Nam Publishers, Glendale, CA, no date.

Bergsma, CDR Herbert L. *Chaplains with Marines in Vietnam 1962-71*. history and Museums Division, Headquarters, USMC, Washington, DC, 1985.

Consolidated Technical Bulletin on Soviet Armor, Department of the Army, Washington, DC, no date.

Kelly, COL Francis. *US Army Special Forces 1961-1971*. Department of the Army, Washington, DC, 1973.

Nalty, Bernard C. *Airpower and the Fight for Khe Sanh*. Office of Air Force History, USAF, Washington, DC, 1973.

Pearson, LTG Willard. *The War in the Northern Provinces 1966-68*. Department of the Army, Washington, DC, 1975.

Schungel, Colonel Daniel F. *After action letter to Colonel Robert E. Ley, chief of Doctrine and Training Division, US Army Armor School, Fort Knox, Kentucky, dated August 8, 1973.*

Shore, Capt. Moyers S. II. *The Battle for Khe Sanh.* History and Museums Division, Headquarters, USMC, Washington, DC, 1969 (reprinted 1977).

Spector, Ronald H. *Advice and Support: The Early Years 1941-1960.* Center for Military History, US Army, Washington, DC, 1983.

Starry, General Donn A. *Mounted Combat in Vietnam.* Department of the Army, Washington, DC, 1978.

Stubbe, Chaplain Ray. *Unpublished notes during the siege of Khe Sanh.* History and Museums Division, Headquarters, USMC, Washington, DC, 1971.

Index

Index to Photographs

Index to Maps

About The Author

Photo courtesy of Amy Stockwell

David B. Stockwell is a U.S. Army Armor Captain who currently maintains command of forces at Fort Knox, Kentucky. Stockwell was born into the military and traveled the U.S., Germany and Turkey, giving flavor to his journalism in later years. He worked as a daily newspaper editor after he earned his bachelor's degree in journalism, and has written for several military trade publications. In fact, *Tanks in the Wire!* began as an article for an Army publication documenting the Battles. But the scope of his idea grew beyond his expectations. "It grew because there is a story to be told and a lesson to be learned," said Stockwell. Hence, the book you hold in your hands is his labor of love for those who died, perhaps needlessly, in Vietnam. Stockwell leaves it to you to draw your own conclusions.